Help the Poor in the Richest City

—The story of Bill Shields

By Zhaoyan Sun and Zhaohan Sun

Canada International Press

Help the Poor in the Richest City
——The story of Bill Shields
Written by: Zhaoyan Sun and Zhaohan Sun
Cover Design: Wen Wen
Editor: Ying Xie
Published by: Canada International Press
www.intlpressca.com
email: service@intlpressca.com

ISBN: 978-1-989763-50-6

Ebook ISBN: 978-1-989763-51-3

Preface

The production of this book is a story of a charity organization. Authors Zhaoyan Sun and Zhaohan Sun are international students who have come to Canada to study. They studied elementary school in China, junior high school and high school in Canada. The two sentiments to the country, especially the civil philanthropy in Canada, are highly recognized because of their participation.

By chance, the youth authors participated in a unique charity organization that provides help to low-income families, especially single-parent families and refugee families. This organization is called "SafetyNet Children and Youth Charity", the founder is Bill Shields. While providing free music lessons for the charity, the young authors have a deeper understanding of Bill and were moved by his life story. They used their spare time to interview Bill and people around him, which experienced rest and blockage during the new crown epidemic.

It is Oakville, the city served by Bill's charity organization, and the richest city in Canada. In the small city, there are still a lot of low-income people who need the help and provision of government authorities and social institutions for their food, clothing, housing and transportation. In this book, the authors expressed such a viewpoint with profound sociological viewpoints:

Whether a country or society is developed does not depend on whether there are poor people, but to effectively think about a reasonable and formulated social medicine to help the poor around oneself effectively.

In developed country Canada, in the richest city Oakville, there is a philanthropist named Bill. He has been involved in philanthropy mergers all his life, gathering the absence of the government, and increasing the society's self-help capabilities.

Bill's story is touching and has spiritual meaning: only by allowing and encouraging social forces to participate in charity can every corner of the sun not shine, and everyone is obscured by the aura of "developed country" and "richest city" people and families in need of assistance receive the most basic and most needed assistance.

Contents

Chapter One

Bill's refugee child, my guitar tutorial

By Zhaoyan Sun

Section One ---- First met with Bill

My younger brother, Zhaohan Sun and I came to Oakville with our parents in August 2016. This is a small city of 100,000 people in Ontario, Canada, 50 kilometers away from downtown Toronto. Dad said that the relationship between Oakville and Toronto is equivalent to the relationship between Suzhou and Shanghai. The former is the back garden of the latter. In fact, the same is true. Oakville has been the wealthiest city in Canada for many consecutive years, and housing prices are also the highest in Canada. Rich people in Toronto choose to settle in Oakville, a beautiful lakeside city.

But no matter how rich the place is, there are poor people, and they are the real poor people who often worry about the necessities of life such as food, clothing, shelter, etc. Our book tells the story of a legendary philanthropist who helped the poor in this small and affluent city. The story of the whole book includes a complete narration and five detailed interviews. It should be very exciting. Please keep reading. Maybe you will feel different.

We came from Beijing, a huge super city, to Oakville, a small lakeside city, and our first impression was to lament the magic and greatness of the Creator. Lake Ontario is really too big, as big as the sea. In fact, there are indeed many scenes and phenomena that can only be found in the ocean. We can see it by the lake. For example, lake gulls are very large, with their wings extended and wider than the arms of seagulls. Every time we come to Lake Ontario and see flocks of gulls flying in the sky, we suspect that we are not really on the

Pacific Ocean or the Atlantic Ocean.

When we were in Beijing, we lived in a fifteen-story high-rise apartment. After we came to Oakville, we lived in a detached house, which is what everyone calls a luxury villa. There are lawns and flower gardens on the front and back of the house. We arrived in midsummer, and the front and back of the house were full of flowers, as if we were welcome. This scene in Beijing, which can only be seen in the park, is now around my home. The beauty of Canada is scattered in every corner of it. Everyone we meet, our friends, classmates, and neighbors, are all beneficiaries of this beautiful environment.

When I first arrived in Canada, I was in seventh grade. According to the school's requirements, my brother and I had to use our spare time to do volunteer work. Our neighbor happened to be a beautiful and young Chinese mother, Wen Yang, her husband Atreya Basu, He is an Indian-Canadian, a computer engineer. Wen Yang took the initiative to introduce us to a charity in Oakville to be a volunteer, she often donated clothes to this charity machine. This is the summer of 2017, the second year we came to Canada.

I vividly remember the day I saw Bill Shields for the first time. Bill is the founder and manager of this charity.

On July 1, 2017, the day of Canada's National Holiday, it seems that the whole of Canada is celebrating the 150th anniversary of the founding of this wealthy country. According to the address, my father drove me to the entrance of a huge warehouse in the Oakville Industrial Zone. There was a less conspicuous sign on the top of the warehouse: SafetyNet Children and Youth Charities. This is it.

Bill opened the door with a smile to welcome us. This is a tall and mighty middle-aged man, about the same age as my father, but much taller than my father. Standing next to his huge warehouse, he is a perfect match. Later I learned that Bill is of Irish descent. When he was young, he went to Ireland to find his roots and ancestors.

After a brief exchange, Bill assigned me to be a guitar teacher to teach refugee children to learn guitar-this is a really good job. It seems that I have seen the effect of my flattery. I said that I am an expert in trumpet performance, and I can also play guitar. Maybe the cost of the trumpet is too high and the refugee children cannot afford it, the guitar is more common and cheap, and it is not difficult to learn. Therefore, there are more people who learn the guitar than the trumpet. I guessed so.

It was soon discovered that our conjecture was correct. Children from refugee families who want to learn guitar are more than we thought.

Maybe Bill was also very happy-he found another guitar teacher. On the day he interviewed me, he posted a photo of me on his social account and welcomed me as a volunteer for this charity. Bill is very humorous, he specially combined me with a picture of a big cock. The cock was standing on top of me, as if he was supervising me: teach the kids how to learn guitar, or I will peck your head.

My parents, and my younger brother are also

very happy. It is not easy to find a volunteer who can give full play to our expertise. When I first looked for volunteer opportunities, I even imagined: Let me help with the baby and change their diapers. Now this volunteer opportunity, I can even regard it as a time for music and entertainment at the same time. It's worth celebrating twice in one fell swoop.

Sure enough, that night, people from all over Canada joined me in celebrating the 150st National Day of Canada, and at the same time celebrating that I found a wonderful volunteer opportunity. I stood in front of the bedroom window on the second floor, watching the blooming fireworks outside the window, listening to the rumble of firecrackers, and reminding myself: I have to spare more time to practice guitar, and I can't let down this volunteer opportunity.

Section Two ---- I was let off by the students

When I first started as a guitar teacher, I ran into trouble: children from refugee families almost always arrived late, or simply stopped coming, and never said hello, let alone apply to me or Bill in advance.

I had just arrived in Canada one year ago, and I am still trying to fit Canada's completely different education system, trying to complete my homework on time. Although the school homework was much less than when I was in China, there were still some to be completed every day, and my homework was very slow at that time. Every time it was a get out of class in the afternoon, my father drove me straight to Bill's charity. According to the pre-arranged arrangement, I had to set aside two afternoons a week to give guitar lessons to four children from refugee families, each for 45 minutes. But what often happens: I rushed to Bill's warehouse, only to find that the students did not come. The better situation is that the students finally came, 20 or 30 minutes late; the worse The situation is: I waited until the time was over and the students did not arrive. Calling, the other party did not answer; writing an email, the other party did not reply, or the next day, simply tell me and Bill: did not get on the bus yesterday, yesterday my dad's car broke down, or said nothing, just say sorry, It won't be too late next time.

But the next time it will be late, and the reason is almost the same as the last time.

The probability of this happening is very high.

Almost a quarter of my time is spent waiting. I hope that my students will arrive on time, just as I am looking forward to an extra reward. My parents and teachers have taught me and my brother from childhood to most of the time, we must be punctual and punctual. Once we have agreed on the time and place with others, don't change it easily, let alone breach the contract without authorization and release each other's pigeons. This is not only Delaying other people's time is more likely to destroy the trust between each other and hurt the feelings between people.

But now I have encountered so many students who are late and absent from the music lessons. How can I solve it? I feel like a desperate refugee, and I need Bill's help.

Bill actually knew about this situation a long time ago. He said that this is not unexpected. Many refugee families come from war-torn countries, as well as from underdeveloped countries. Under the difficult living conditions, what they care most about is to obtain the most basic life resources. Now when they come to Canada, they can offer their children to participate in various educational poverty alleviation projects, including guitar training, within a very short period of time. This in itself shows that they have a strong desire to change the lifestyle of the next generation through education. But this kind of change cannot be completed overnight. It needs to start with every seemingly trivial detail. For example, in Canada and China, punctuality, respect for agreements, and not easy to change plans, these basic rules of conduct will be a little uncomfortable when they are implemented. We need to work harder and show more patience. Remind them, ask them, and help them make changes in these areas. We help them develop these habits, which is also an act of charity.

Bill went on to say: Of course, if they insist on not changing, we can't just accommodate them, we can't allow them to be late and absent from school all the time, otherwise it will delay your time and affect other refugee family children. Bill gave a specific standard: If three times cumulatively, if he does not come to class without saying hello or applying, he will cancel the opportunity for the child to participate in guitar training.

I think Bill's words are extremely correct. His idea of "three unexcused absenteeism will be disqualified for training" is also a great idea. But I did not expect that the first student recruited was an excellent student, a seventh-grade girl from Syria. In order to protect her privacy, we will call her Joan for the time being. She was first cancelled by Bill. Qualified for study. I feel a little sorry about this, this should not be Joan's fault, but should be attributed to her father's non-punctuality. Joan is a beautiful girl. Every time she comes to class, she wears a headscarf of different colors. She works very hard when she learns the guitar, but the foundation is really a bit poor and she basically doesn't understand the staff. But Joan is very smart, and as soon as I teach, she will. When she was late for the second time, I reminded her: If you are late again, you may not be able to learn guitar with me.

She was shocked, and then told me cautiously: Her father didn't buy a car, and every time she came to class, she came by bus. When they came to class last time, their family had two bicycles for the first time. But home should be quite far from here. It takes too long to ride a bike to class, and it is also very tiring.

On the way back, I told my father about the fact that Joan's house does not have a car, which surprised him a bit. In Canada, especially in a small city like Oakville with only about 100,000 people, it is almost impossible to move without a car. To clarify this issue, we have to start with the concept of "small cities".

The concept of small cities in Canada is completely different from the concept of small cities in China. Small cities with about 100,000 people in China are generally county towns. The population is concentrated around a few crisscross streets. The housing is mostly multi-story buildings with five to ten stories. Now the local economy is developed. Ten-story buildings are not uncommon. Everyone gathers together, or to put it more vividly, the population of small cities in China live and live together. The land utilization rate is extremely high. There are shopping malls and supermarkets downstairs, and restaurants, hair salons, game halls, and movie theaters are nearby. The elementary school is just in front of the home, and the middle school is no more than five kilometers away; many of the uncle's, aunt's, grandpa's, and grandma's homes also live in the neighbor community. So whether you are an adult or a child, go to work, school, relatives and friends, you can walk straight away, and ride a bicycle far away, and you will be there in a while, if you are not in a hurry, you can sit leisurely in a few places and stop where you want to go.

Canada is different. Dad always said: Canada is a country that is flat on the ground. Almost all private houses and public buildings are flat and spread out on the vast North American land. As far as the eye can see, the most seen are one or two-story buildings, occasionally there are some multi-story buildings, and very few high-rise buildings over a dozen stories are seen. The front and back of the private house are spacious and beautiful private gardens, and the front and the back of the public buildings are neatly arranged and there are plenty of parking spaces. The arrangement of ground buildings in this way results in an extremely large area for any small city in Canada. For example, Oakville where we live now, a small city of about 100,000 people. The total population of the district, the latest statistics in 2021 is 3.5 million.

Living in such a huge "small city", if you don't have a car, you will find it extremely difficult to even buy some daily necessities. Of course there are buses, but because there are too few customers, the number of trains is sparse. If you want to take a bus to work or school, you need to spend several times longer, and you have to be patient enough to ensure that you will not be late.

Therefore, if the father of Syrian refugee Joan does not have a car, it is difficult to guarantee that his daughter will not be late for class. Thinking of this, I also feel very helpless. Bill has done enough for refugees, including Joan, to provide them with clothes, furniture and music education. You can never expect Bill to provide them with cars for free.

Section Three ---- Free Bicycles

It is true that Bill cannot provide free cars to refugee families living in the affluent Oakville, but he can provide them with free bicycles, and he also provides a lot, benefiting thousands of families.

Now is 2018, and there are still two years before I can test for a driver's license in Canada. So every time I go to Bill's charity warehouse, I have to trouble my dad to drive me. When I was taking guitar lessons, he ran to the innermost corner of the warehouse and chatted with Chil. Chil is a young Chinese and a computer expert. He has been a volunteer in Bill's warehouse for a long time. His role here is a bicycle repair expert.

I need to describe this huge warehouse in Bill. It is a rectangular single warehouse with an internal space of about 3,000 square meters. The front is about 300 square meters is the reception area, office area and clothing finishing area. Later, I used it as a performance area and auditorium for guitar solo concerts. Next is the clothing and kitchen utensils area, about 500 square meters. Further down there is the furniture area and the mattress area. This area occupies the largest area and has the most inventory, and it often encroaches on the territory of other areas. If more furniture and mattresses are donated, the sites in other areas will be borrowed, at least 1,000 To 1,500 square meters.

Passing through the mountain of furniture area and cushion area, you will arrive at the innermost bicycle area. This area, like the furniture area, often expands or shrinks the site due to the amount of donations. Generally maintained at about 500 square meters. You can imagine how many bicycles in an area of 500 square meters.

The most popular item in Bill's warehouse is mattresses. Bill once briefly introduced it to me, all of these mattresses are brand new, not second-hand. The second most popular is clothes. Because it is so popular, Bill has made strict rules: on a person-by-person basis, each person who comes to choose clothes can only choose four clothes at most.

The third most popular item is the bicycle.

In order to ensure sufficient quantities of the three categories of "furniture and mattresses, clothes and kitchen supplies, and bicycles", Bill tried his best. We will talk about this story later. After these three types of items enter the warehouse, everything is not all right. Clothes need to be sorted, furniture needs to be repaired and installed, bicycles are the most troublesome, and it takes a lot of time and energy to repair, replace old and broken parts, reinforce and upgrade the brake system to ensure the safety of cyclists.

For each of the above items, a group of volunteers are needed to help Bill. The simplest clothes are classified by adults and children, then by gender, then by spring, summer, autumn, and winter, and finally by the degree of newness and oldness. The furniture is cumbersome, heavy and big, and several strong people are needed to help it in and out. However, these jobs do not have high requirements for technology and ability. Only bicycle repairs require very high professional skills.

Chil's bicycle repair skills are very high, and he is a well-deserved "bicycle king". When I was giving guitar lessons to students, I often saw my dad passing by on a newly repaired bicycle. Whenever this time, my dad was also working as a volunteer, helping Chil test the bicycle.

Once Dad was riding on a big and tall vintage bicycle and didn't want to get off. He kept riding through rainforest-like clothing, furniture, and mattresses. Gill followed behind, holding a large one in his hand, moving his hands and fine-tuning the parts on the bike at any time. My guitar lessons are over, and the two of them are still enthusiastically discussing this old-style black bicycle that looks like it just rode out of an old movie.

On the way back, my father told me that this bicycle was indeed ridden from 70 years ago. This is the oldest bicycle brand in the UK, Raleigh, which means noble, fresh and cute. The bicycle repaired by Gill is a product of the British Raleigh Bicycle Company in the 1950s. It has been seventy years ago, and it has only been 150 years since the emergence of a bicycle with a chain and transmission in the true modern sense.

Next time I went to class, I deliberately went to the innermost bicycle area of the warehouse and visited this grandpa bicycle. This is a bicycle for man. The handlebars are horizontal and straight, just like the bicycles in the old movies. The front is inlaid with a beautiful company nameplate. The seat is made of leather. The most surprising thing is that this bike is a sporty bike with variable speeds, and after Chil's meticulous repairs, the performance of the transmission seventy years ago is no worse than that of the current latest transmission. No wonder Dad was reluctant to get off after riding it, he is a PhD in history, and he is naturally interested in ancient things; if this thing happens to be able to function, then he will love it even more.

Let me ask Chil first: This Raleigh bicycle that took you several days to repair, looks like a nobleman in the bicycle family, was it very expensive at the time? Is it very valuable now? Chil thought for a while and said: In the 1950s, Canadians who owned a Raleigh variable speed bicycle must be high-income people; now this bicycle can be said to be particularly valuable. I believe many bicycle collectors are looking for such bike. A high-end bicycle that can be used normally could be sold at a high price; but it can also be said that it is not worth a penny. If I repair it, it does not belong to me. Bill will give it to them for free, the first person to apply for a bicycle.

A few days later, when I went to the bicycle workshop to check it again, the old bicycle that was rejuvenated with youth was gone-it was taken by a lucky grantee. I found Bill and asked: Do you know the value of this bicycle? It is very valuable. Bill seemed to have forgotten the bicycle he had mentioned during the chat before. He laughed and made a trademark grimace-his left eye was open, his right eye was squeezed twice, and he said: We don't make movies, we don't need Good-looking classic cars, you only need bicycles that can be ridden. A bicycle can bring joy and convenience to its owner, and it is the most precious thing.

Section Four ---- Electric Bicycle

Bill's bicycle brings joy to many people. So, what can bring joy to Bill himself?

The answer may surprise you: it is also a bicycle, but it must be electric.

When I was giving guitar lessons to my students, if it was just in time for Bill to leave work late and there was nothing else, Dad would go to Bill's office and chat with him. I knew that this was because Dad was consciously looking for English as his mother tongue. People practice spoken English. Dad's English is poor, but his learning enthusiasm is very high.

For a while, my father was busy searching the Internet for information on electric bicycles. It turned out that when Bill was chatting with him— that is, when he was taking a free oral English class, he told him that his hobby is to go out on an electric bicycle; he heard that the quality of electric bicycles in China is very high and the price is very low. Just ask my dad. Can you buy one directly from an electric bicycle factory in China, and then ship it to Canada by sea?

Dad promised that electric bicycles are particularly popular in China, especially in super-large cities like Beijing, Shanghai, and Shenzhen, with a population of 20-30 million. The traffic is always busy and congested. Many people drive. The speed of walking is slower than walking; if you ride a bicycle, it may be faster; but when it is cold, riding a bicycle will feel like reaching the North Pole; riding a bicycle on a hot day will feel like reaching the equator. Electric bicycles solve these two problems very well: they will not be blocked in the middle of the road and cannot move, and they will not be trembling with cold in the winter and hot in the summer due to hard riding.

We have lived in Canada for so long, and we have hardly seen electric bicycles. The most common electric vehicle is a Tesla electric car that passes by you, and the other is an electric car traveling leisurely on the golf course. Dad is very supportive of Bill's "playing with electric bicycles". He told me: Everyone has to have a hobby. Like Bill, the guy who spends almost his entire life and all his money and energy on charity also has to have a little bit of his own life. According to Chinese standards, Bill is a living Lei Feng.

Speaking of Lei Feng, my dad then introduced to me: If viewed by international standards, Lei Feng is the most well-known philanthropist in China. He was born in 1940, suffered a car accident, and died in 1962. In his short life, he did countless good things to help people. After his death, Chairman Mao Zedong made an inscription for him: Learn from Comrade Lei Feng. As a result, Lei Feng became the most famous and officially recognized philanthropist in China's history. In China, Lei Feng is already deified and sanctified. However, some historical details that were later confirmed proved that even Lei Feng, who was uninterested and special in the Chinese impression, likes leather coats and also has high-end watches. This detail was revealed only decades after Lei Feng's death.

Dad compared Bill to "Living Lei Feng", which is a particularly interesting point. In China, if you want to praise someone who is helpful and charitable, it's like this. Those who are praised will certainly feel very happy.

"Living Lei Feng" wanted an electric bicycle, and my dad was very eager to help him realize this not extravagant wish. After some comparisons, he helped Bill choose an electric bicycle factory in Shenzhen, an industrial city in southern China. After communicating via emails, the other party sent a bunch of product photos. After repeated comparisons, Bill chose a retro electric bicycle. The style is also like a ride from an old movie. The factory price is 880 Canadian dollars. There is no electric bicycle of the same model in Canada. Similar products are offered in Canada at about 1800 Canadian dollars.

Once the idea is turned into reality, difficulties will follow one after another. It is not expensive to buy electric bicycles in China, However, the time and transportation costs of transporting electric bicycles from China to Canada are ridiculously high. It takes two months to ship a complete vehicle from southern China to Ontario, Canada, and the price needs about 2,000 Canadian dollars. In this way, it is much more expensive than buying in Canada. In this way, Bill and my dad discussed with each other for about two months. Bill's biggest gain was to understand the international market of electric bicycles, and my dad's biggest gain was to improve his oral English. I think if Bill wanted my dad to buy a four-wheeled car instead of a two-wheeled electric bicycle, his oral English would be doubled.

Section Five ---- Christmas concert

The guitar course prescribed by Bill is three months long; a group of students will be changed every three months. If the original students still want to continue their studies, they can continue to sign up and follow me to practice guitar.

There is a little girl from Venezuela, let's call her Silvia for the time being, who followed me to learn guitar for two sessions. Silvia is just ten years old this year. She is a chubby girl with a round face and comes from a refugee family. Unlike the images of malnourished and scrawny African refugees that Chinese people have seen in newspapers and TV before, the refugees I have seen from the Middle East and South America, especially their children, such as Silvia, are rarely malnourished. Existing, many children seem to have over-nutrition. This may be the general gap between developed and underdeveloped countries.

Silvia studies very hard. Although she is about the same level as guitar and not much basic music knowledge, she has a high enthusiasm for learning, and her parents are more responsible than Joan's parents and have never been late. Of course, it is related to having a hatchback at her home.

When Silvia comes to school, she is usually driven by her mother. Her mother is very polite, thanking me, Bill and my father every time, and then staying aside in silence, watching her daughter play the guitar intently with affectionate eyes. . Bill's theory is correct. Many low-income families and refugee families have consciously improved their children's education level to break through the inherent classes and circles so that their children can lead a more quality and decent life.

Several times, Silvia's mother brought several of her family and friends to Bill's charity warehouse to watch my guitar lessons. Each of them looked attentive, as if Silvia was not playing monotonous etudes, but wonderful joy in the world. I had a whim: just give Silvia a "guitar concert". I told Bill my thoughts, and his squinted eyes suddenly widened:

"Okay, this is a great idea, what do I need to do?"

At this time, there is still more than a month before Christmas in 2019. I, Bill, and Silvia's mother have jointly agreed to set the "Silvia Personal Guitar Concert" at 6pm on December 20th, which happens to be Friday. You can invite More people to attend. The performance location is at the entrance area of the Bill Charity Hall.

When I have a goal, I have motivation. When I teach, I pay more attention to the expressiveness of music than usual, and remind Silvia to pose more professionally. Silvia is also looking forward to the first concert in her life. I believe that most people have never had such an opportunity to show themselves. I noticed that she has started to pay attention to her dress. Every time she comes to class, she wears different clothes. It seemed like they were rehearsing for a concert not long after. This may be her mother's idea, but what does it matter? For a refugee girl of about ten years old, it is a rare quality education and habit formation in itself.

I determined the repertoire of the concert in advance: a total of four pieces, one of which was played by me and Silvia. I first taught Silvia to play two general guitar etudes. This is basic training and can also show her hard work. I also taught her a chord to sing while playing, which is a Canadian folk song. In the end, I played a Chinese traditional song "Jasmine" with her. It was a simplified version of course. I played the main melody and she played the chorus.

Time flies, and the concert arrives in no time. At 4:30 pm on December 20th, my father and I arrived at the performance. Bill also attached great importance to it. He asked a volunteer to set up the performance venue early and moved the finishing platform that had previously been in the front of the hall to the corner, and moved almost all the chairs, stools and sofas in the warehouse to the front. The hall is arranged in two semicircles and surrounds the painted performance area. I noticed that Bill also changed the huge Canadian flag he had hung in front of the clothing area to the back of the performance area, forming a bright stage background.

Just after 5:00, Silvia's relatives and friends came one after another. Before the performance at 6:00, the two rows of auditoriums in front of the performance area were full. Everyone was wearing formal attire, although no men wore ties or women. Evening gowns, but everyone dressed beautifully, creating a festive atmosphere. Regrettably, I rushed over directly from the school's badminton team, wearing Under Armour sportswear. I counted it, and about thirty people came. Such a large group of relatives and friends of "refugee families' ' surprised me-are they all refugees from Venezuela? Can a foreign family in South America relocate to Canada in North America as a whole? Thinking of this level, I feel more and more that Canada is a country of great tolerance, multicultural, multi-ethnic, and harmonious coexistence. The national characteristics of Canada that I learned in my civics class are now vividly displayed in my mind.

The performance began, and Bill also withdrew from his busy schedule and came to the audience. Standing behind Silvia's grandparents, he greeted them enthusiastically.

First of all, I made an opening remark. I greatly praised Silvia's learning enthusiasm and her musical talent, and briefly introduced the repertoire that will be performed today. Then I asked Silvia to introduce herself to her learning process over the past few months. The little girl was very generous and said that she liked playing guitar, but her fingers were a little sore, and everyone laughed.

The performance went more smoothly than I thought. Silvia played seriously. Her parents and grandparents listened carefully. I even saw her father wipe the corners of his eyes a few times, perhaps because of the excitement.

But the four pieces are too short. The performance was over all at once. It seemed that it was over before it started. It seemed that the applause time at the end was longer than the performance time. Silvia and I are a little reluctant, but she really has no other songs to play.

Section Six ---- Chocolate and red wine gifts

Doing charity work is not entirely selfless giving and dedication. Many times you will encounter surprises and rewards. For example, in the big boxes on the shelf in front of Bill's office, you will never think of what kind of good things will be inside.

My guitar teaching job is usually twice a week, Tuesday and Friday. Every Friday, the students will increase by one or two, so the end time will be extended to 7:30 in the evening. At half past seven in summer, the sky was still bright; but at half past seven in winter, it was as dark as midnight. Canada has a very high latitude. The latitude of Toronto is approximately equal to the latitude of Shenyang in northeastern China, so the days in winter are particularly short.

Every Friday, Bill leaves work earlier than usual, so my father is responsible for turning off the warehouse lights and locking the warehouse doors every time. After the students have left, the huge warehouse filled with clothes, furniture, mattresses, and bicycles looks complicated and mysterious. Coupled with the boundless silence and deep darkness in the middle of the winter night in North America, there will be a place in the warehouse. This kind of inexplicable tension and fear, what you want most at this time is that besides someone by your side, there may be delicious chewing in your mouth.

Bill may also be aware of the loneliness and desertedness in the warehouse at night. He once reminded me in particular: On the top of the kitchen shelf, there is a row of blue storage boxes. If you are hungry or greedy, you can open the boxes to find them. Find it-you won't be disappointed.

Before Bill's voice fell, I felt hungry, but the guitar class was not over yet, and I had to wait for the students to leave before I could solve the problem of gluttony.

The student finally left. Dad helped me find a ladder. I climbed to the three-meter-high shelf, opened the blue box, and yelled "Wow": Most of the boxes of bulk chocolates have brands I am familiar with, there are varieties that I haven't seen. I heard Bill said before that donors sometimes donate small things that give people surprises. Probably this is what he calls surprises. This is an exclusive benefit that practitioners in other industries have no chance to enjoy.

With chocolate, the warehouse at night no longer looks lonely and deserted in an instant. While enjoying the delicious chocolate, my father and I are looking forward to the early arrival of the next guitar class.

There is an old saying in China: reciprocity and reciprocity. It means that if someone gives you a gift, you should give it back to someone at the right time, so that the friendship between you and the other person can be long and your interpersonal relationship has to be harmonious. My dad and I ate the delicious chocolate that Bill collected in the top layer of the Hejia-this is regarded as a gift to us. According to ancient Chinese traditions and international diplomatic practices, we also want to give him value and meaning in return.

Chapter two

"You're just so wrapped up in that wheel"

——Interview with Bill Shields
By Zhaoyan Sun and Zhaohan Sun

Sun(S):   Congratulations to your charity, a new place has been added. Can you introduce this new place?

Bill(B): Yeah, now we have another place for lessons, it's an another place where we're doing tutoring and music lessons in September 2021.

S: During the COVID-19 epidemic, there are new developments in your charity, which is surprising. Does the epidemic affect your affairs?

B: So it's over the frontier and spheres. But for the first 3 months of this pandemic, we were deemed an essential service, I had to run it on my own. So we had to let all the volunteers and the staff. So it was very hard. We stayed open for clothing and for diapers and furniture. We really got hit hard by demand. We have people start coming in who thought they would never visit a charity, they got hit by the pandemic. I go home every night. It was very hard work because you went home and I was scared. I would be questioning myself: Did I get too close to somebody? Did I contract the disease? Am I bringing it(virus) home? It was a very tough time. And in those days, when the people were saying that COVID-19 was spread by contact, I'd be spraying things down, cleaning them. When someone comes in for diapers, I make sure they're far away, but it still has a lasting effect on me.

Now people get close automatically back off and, so it had a pretty big effect on you know what I mean. But we stayed busier now. We're I think we're close to 5,000 families that we're right now. Yeah. But we're starting music and tutoring again at the new place.

S: Where is the location of your new music department?

B: Just up the street. So we've got another place that's just dedicated to tutoring and music and. It's got glass rooms and it's in Oakville.

S: How 's the total area of the new department?

B: It's got four separate rooms, four glass rooms, and it's about maybe about 1,000 square feet.

S: When will the new department start operating?

B: It's mainly dedicated to tutoring. Hopefully it will be in use in September or October, depending on the effect of Delta (Covid-19 delta variant); the state is a mess right now. I don't know if it affects us the way it did before. We're more vaccinated here. I don't know.

S: Okay, let's get back to business, starting from your childhood. Could you tell us about your family?

B: Until the age of 8 , I had my mother and father, my father left when I was the age of 8. I was the only child in my school that was from a broken home. My father did have alcohol-related problem; I don't know if that was the cause of what happened. I had one sister. My family did take a hit in the 1970s when my father left. I see him a bit, but not often, we didn't have the closest relationship.

S: When your dad first left your family, how did you cope with his departure?

B: It didn't hit me as hard as it did to my sister and my mother, my sister was 2 years older than me. I don't think at the time I consciously felt much. I think later in life, it had its effects on me. Later in life, I realized it would have been nice to have a father around when I was younger. My father may not have had the tool to be there for me all the time. At the time, I don't recall it having a big effect on me. Later in life, it did. I think when I was in my 20s, I blamed him for not being there with me. But now that I'm mature. I can look back and be forgiving. Because a person can only act to the level they're at. Right? So you can't expect somebody who has a broken leg to run the 100 Mile dash. You can't expect that out of them. You can't blame them. People can only do what they're capable of doing. I don't blame them, and now I'm very good with it. I understand that he might have had some problems back then.

S: Do you have any sort of memorable things that you did with your father?

B: No, we didn't have that kind of relationship. Like I just took my 8-year-old son on a fishing trip for a week. We did some good fishing, but I didn't have that with my father when he was still around. And I must say, I probably wasn't there enough for my first son. But this time with my 8-year-old son, I'm very much involved. I was very much there. I just got another electric bike from China. He rides on the back and that so I made sure I spent that time with them. I don't have any old memories of my father whatsoever. None of those things.

S: Had your father contributed anything to the family before he left?

B: I can't really remember him doing anything with us, to be honest with you. I don't remember having those memories with my father. I don't have that. I play hockey with my son Billy all the time and I'm teaching Billy how to box. But I didn't do any of that stuff with my father. I had none of that.

S: After your dad left, your mother raised your sister and you all alone?

B: Back then, my mom didn't get a lot of support from her husband. She worked two jobs. She would leave at 8 am, generally she would come back at 10 in the night. a lot of times she was able to do something to get home at 6 and work at home doing digital typing. She worked as a medical secretary. She did two jobs to support us, which is very hard for her. So in a lot of ways we had to be responsible to take care of ourselves.

S: Do you have good rapport with your mother? .

B: Definitely, my mother worked two or three jobs to raise us I think, and in a lot of ways we raised ourselves too. She took us camping, she spent time with us. Back then, I was a very hard child to raise; I got kicked out of the house because I could be violent when I was young, back then I was around 15 or 16. I got kicked out of the house sometimes. Sometimes I punched walls and I'd lose my temper, so I was a very hard child to raise. She did her best. She didn't have all the skills either. I think the way she handled things is never the way I would have handled them, but what she had she did her best. I think in some ways, her way of educating forced me to be a rebel.

I can remember when I was 15, my friend was having a party and everybody was going there, so I said to my mother that I'd really like to go. She said no, she was saying right away, she didn't trust that. I act that way properly. I was kind of ostracized for it. Then I think certain stuff started to make me angry and I think not having a father made me angry and so I would lash out.

But she did what she could with the skills she had and she did a good job. When the chips were down, I really needed my mother, she would be there. Did she kick me out of the house a few times? Yes. Did I sleep outside a few times when I was 15 or 16? Yes. But she was doing the best she could with an angry kid.

S: And how long did your mother work for the two or three jobs that you mentioned?

B: She worked until the age of 70, I think. Even after I became an adult, she was still working. My father left her nothing. My father left our family nothing. No, and he didn't really help us as much as she should have and she had to work. She didn't have a pension; she didn't have any savings. We were lucky that we had my grandmother's house because we lived with my grandmother, and I can remember my mother being late with the rent, but with my grandmother, so we were okay, but my grandmother is very patient with us. Yeah. But again, I grew up in the same house. My mother grew up there, right? So now my father didn't do as much as she should have.

S: Which three jobs did she work for?

B: She was a medical secretary, okay? Then at night she did Dictaphone typing for two different doctors. Sometimes she would do it from home, sometimes she stayed at the office, right? A lot of times she would do it from home, so she could be home. It was a struggle.

S: After you became an adult, did you move to another place far away from your mother?

B: I traveled a lot and I lived in England for a while but I think no, I've always been in proximity with my mother. We've always been pretty close. In fact, my mother's coming up Thursday for a week.

S: So, you and your mother were connected the entire time?

B: Connected. Absolutely. The only one I have no connection with is my sister. Yeah, so I have no connection with her whatsoever.

S: Could you talk about your Early Education, where you went to school for middle school and high school?

Bill: I went to school from kindergarten to grade six in Edith vale Public School now it is in Willow dale, and it was very small community then Toronto wasn't as big in fact until the age of seven finches was a dirt road, but my experience at Edith vale was very good, it was very carefree times when I went to elementary school. There was a creek that ran beside the school. I didn't do outstanding in school, I didn't apply myself a whole lot. I think in later years I found I had somewhat of a learning disability, which now they probably call dyslexic.

But I found the school and teaching rather boring and I didn't focus a lot. My face will be out the window half the time when school is going on. But then I remember I had a lot of good friends and we play road hockey every day; we also hide and seek after school. Most of my time is spent outside playing in those days, I did enjoy those days.

The junior high school I went to a school called RJ Lange for grades 7 8 and 9 and I didn't particularly like it. Same with high school I didn't feel like I fit in a whole lot. I wasn't a very click guy. In grades 7 8 and 9, it was more survival for me. It wasn't I particularly enjoyed and again in junior high and high school, I didn't particularly apply myself. I started smoking a grade 7, so I hung around a place called smokers fence when I was in junior high school because back then grade 7 you could smoke.

I probably hung out with some of the wrong people and I probably was one the wrong person myself. I mean we got into Mischief I never got arrested or anything like that but we certainly did cause mischief. I can't say that I particularly enjoyed RJ Lang or North view Heights where I went to high school which is at Bathurst Street and Finch Avenue. again you know I just I didn't feel like I fit in with a whole lot of people. I was in my little world. I mean I knew everybody and had my share of fistfights. I can't say the experience was very pleasant.

S: Last time you mentioned that when you were in grade seven, grade eight, you had a little bit of reading difficulties, is that correct?

B: Yes. Back then it was called learning disability. I was exempted from some classes because of that, I was too young to really know how it manifested. I just know like I didn't have to do typing in some other classes because it really affected my writing. And when I read, I would drop a line here and there?

S: Do you still have that kind of disability?

B: Yes, absolutely, my writing is terrible. But I've learned different ways to overcome it. I think now they would call it dyslexia, I would think. Back then they really didn't have the term. I probably had an attention deficit as well.

S: So did it affect your career?

B: Not at all. I never excelled at college or university or at high school. I never excelled. Here I am. You know what I mean? I got by.

S: While you're in high school or even in elementary school, were you thinking about doing work like this charitable work you are doing today?

B: I didn't think of it then; I didn't think of the future much back then. I never really gave a thought to the next day, not at all wouldn't even be considered back then. To be honest, I didn't have a lot of anybody directing me; I didn't have

a father right so I didn't have anybody directing

me in the right direction。

S: What kind of advice will you get to single parent families in terms of their education, especially in terms of post-high school level education?

B: I think they have to use all resources they can to get their kids educated. That's why we do Free tutoring here. I think education opens your mind. It opens you to the world, okay? And I do suggest they learn in colleges and universities, maybe more colleges now because college people are getting the jobs, right. The children will need to learn skills. Skills right now are very important. Because there's a lack of people doing skills right now. So whatever it is, you would need to get something to break that cycle of poverty. A better way of putting it is to be better than your parents, and excel more, right? But no matter what it is, just break that cycle.

S: Did you attend college after high school?
B: I took a year off and made London my home base and hitchhikes around Ireland Scotland went to France travelling back then. When I came back I decided to go to college and applied to get into college and that's when I

went to social service. That was the time of my life. That's what I came into fruition. I was doing what I wanted to do, I was the vice president of our class. I led a demonstration at the time soon I became politically involved in the world. I demonstrated against certain things like the anti-nuclear movements and I began to raise awareness of feminism and women's rights in college. I expanded my horizons and I was in my element.

S: When you're in a single-parent family, what is the thing you are missing the most?

B: I would think a male influence is the most important. I don't think I had any direction. I think I came a bit out of control behaviorally because I didn't have anyone to lead me to the right direction. I thought it would have been for having that male influence. I never had that and then I think that gives you a bit of stability as a boy at the house.

S: Did any people in your community help your family out in any way we were on our own?

B: No, we were on our own and in those days you don't talk about it; my family is Irish Catholic but when you're Irish Catholic but you don't get divorced so we kind of left the church when we're about 8 after my father left because everybody kind of knew. We lost our support back then.

S: Back in the days, if a charity like Safetynet existed would your life be different?

B: No, back then I don't think my mother would have reached out for help. It would make a difference if it was there and she used it.

S: As you mentioned last time, you mentioned that you were the only child at your school that grew up in an incomplete family. Has the current percentage of incomplete families gone up over the years?

B: I think separated families are the majority, I would think. Maybe it's a 50:50, but back when I was a kid, we were the only ones. I think that's what made me a rebel. I rebelled against religion. To this day I still do because I think religion did that to us? Like you're one of them, right? I rebelled against institutions because we were seen as differently. Oh, and I found it really hard to be judgmental, I have friends who were gay. It would never have occurred me back then when it wasn't accepted in Canada to be prejudiced against somebody for their color or for being gay or whatever. Because I knew it was like to be pointed out that I've always been for the underdog for that reason but. It made me rebellious for sure. Not outwardly when I was in high school as much but when I got to college I became a protester. I protested against things that I thought were wrong. You know what I mean?

S: So it was in your college time that you decided in the future you would want to contribute to the community like you are doing now?

B: When I was doing social service I really became involved in the world. I would think some of my childhood affected my choice, I just wasn't aware of it then. I didn't have the maturity in high school or Junior High School. My best friend, when I was 18, threw himself off the top of the building so I think that's what made me socially involved and wanting to help people. It had quite an impact on me. I still remember to that day; it was about two months after John Lennon was assassinated. I got to work and I just left about half an hour before him, went downtown and we were having fun. I was working at the local Kmart similar to Walmart today. I left him half an hour at the train station, Sheppard Subway, I got to work and my sister called me and said he just committed suicide. so it was quite a blow you know and I think that influenced me a lot into going to social service.

S: Was your initial motivation for starting this charity kind of similar, then like what you did in those protests?

B: Yeah, I think so. I think I thought for people and I think some of it was ego. I think the more mature I get I realized some of my motivation in my 30s and in my 40s was ego as well. Let's be honest with each other. You know what I mean, like I wanted to build something that was the best. I wanted to build something that was big. You know what I mean. That's not important to me anymore. I think. Now my motivations are a little more, really honestly helping people and bringing them out of a certain amount of poverty and emphasizing with people. I think everything from our childhood up leads us in a certain direction for sure. And it had something to do with it. Absolutely. I think for the most part, my intentions were, we're good.

S: So from this pandemic, are you getting more funding from people since they realized the rising demand of charities?

B: We did get more funding, we did get more help, absolutely like things. Some people did step up, like the Oakville community foundation really helped us out. One part of Halton region. When you deal with funders from Halton region, it's just a pain. It really is. They want this, prove that, but we needed it. So they weren't very helpful. But the Oakville community foundation was very helpful at the time. And some other organizations step forward.

S: How much funding did you get from them?

B: I think maybe around 60,000 from them, I think. Yeah, I have some. they were very helpful. How do you say some money? Keep this place open for. We use it to a higher, higher, and stuff is not volunteer right here. We use it to help with stopping mostly to help with staffing, because we came so busy. We rank the volunteers who didn't want to come in, and I can't blame them first, because there's this pandemic, like literally from February or late February. To the end of May. I was doing this. At the end I committed my own. It was weird. Little frightening, you come in on spears and there'll be nobody on it. And it was dreary to come in here. The community foundation really helped out.

S: Has the supplies ever run low in the charity?

B: No, we've done very well throughout, we didn't run short on any supplies. We did very well that way. Yes.

S: Last time you mentioned that you were involved in the feminist protest, is that correct?

B: Yes, during my college time, I protested against many things, not just women's rights. I was on the front page of the sun and the star for protesting. Yeah, it was anti-apartheid. I was very much against the apartheid move. I was also anti-nuclear. And I was pro-feminism, I've been a part of Greenpeace. The reason why I participated the feminist movement was very much about a woman I've fallen in love with. She was a feminist. And she sort of introduced me the idea of pro-feminism. So my own I was anti-apartheid and anti-nuclear. But when this woman came into my life, who I fell head over heels for, she was a feminist and very much got me involved in the feminist movement. I used to go on protests with her a lot. So I did really believe in it, but she introduced me. And one of my college professors introduced me to feminism.

S: Were you like a leader of a group during the protest?

B: It's like, I would have been one of the leaders for sure I remember. There was me and another guy who were kind of the leaders. We had taken over politics, we were protesting the way college teachers were being treated, and the teachers went on strike. At the time, Betty Stevenson was the education minister. We did a protest. We took over her office. We did a sit in. There was me and this other guy who were kind of the leaders, the secretary said, I have to go to the washroom. In the washroom, this was the office, it was over there. She said, can you guys just leave the office? And go into the other door, close the door and go to the washroom? I just want my privacy. The other guy said, no. I said, yes. He goes, no, we're not. I said we will. There are seven other people with us. I said, we're gonna give her privacy and he said, no, I went to walk out. Everybody followed me. So I think by then I was kind of established as a bit of the leader at the time. But then we came back and we did the sit-in. Then we were on the front page of the sun, the star and everything.

It was during the teacher's college strike that we chose to support the teachers. So I was a leader who I was just saying, I can play the guitar and played songs. Yeah, I was speaking of the Beatles. I was very much influenced by John Lennon. You know. He's too young to remember John Lennon was a protest against the Vietnam war. Yeah.

S: Work participating in that demonstration.

B: That I remember the one it's a long time ago, there's always lots of people on the demonstrations where there was anti-nuclear, anti-apartheid. In those, I just took part of them. I wasn't really as much a leader then. But in the college ones, there were thousands of people at Queens Park. What have you? They were big demonstrations back then? Yeah. I remember when the American invaded Iraq, that was the last demonstration I went to, and we went downtown to the American consulate. I think that was 2002 when George Bush invaded Iraq, and we demonstrated the game step. But when we went down there, and there were only about 30 or 40 people, I said, maybe the times have changed, maybe protests aren't the way to go anymore.

S: Was the social atmosphere around that time very different from right now?

B: Yes, it is very different from now. I'm not saying my generation is better or worse. But people I think were more socially conscious back then. But then if you look at places and I think we were forced into it, there was more that was affecting us. So I think people in certain parts of the Middle East are more politically conscious because of what's going on around them. But I think certain times lead to being more socially conscious. I wonder how this pandemic is going to affect my 8 and 12-year-old. Are they gonna be more political? Are they gonna be more socially conscious because of this? Furthermore, I think people now have become more isolated. I do. And I think there's a lot less camaraderie. But then I would question myself how much did we change like a lot of the people who protested along with me? They're not the same people. But I think all that is meaningless in a sense that sometimes the more we fight things, the bigger they become. I'm kind of learning that.

I think if you want to change the world, you have to change yourself. I I think our job is sort of to lose the ego and become more conscious. I don't know if that makes sense. You know you have thoughts. And thought goes like clouds, they go from me all the time. We mistake our thoughts for who we are. Who we are is the observer of the thoughts. I think we have to become more in touch with the observer, with the conscience of who we are, not the scattering that's going on by us. And I think that's important, like I meditate, and I think that's important. If you want to change things, you have to change yourself.

S: Do you still meditate now?

B: Yes, I meditate 3 times a day currently.

S: Does meditation provide you significant help for calming yourself down?

B: Big time. It really helps. But then again, people meditate for different reasons. I think it depends on your motivation too. If I'm having a day where everything is going around me like if I were to be standing while three people asking me something, three things going on at once. The phones are ringing, and when I cannot focus. I would meditate and focus on one thing at a time. It really helps. And I also think this rapid exposure of information is bad for this generation. You got your phone ring and you got social media, you've got text going on. We're not meant for that. And don't get me wrong. I'm not knocking your generation. I'm definitely not. Everybody has to learn what they need to learn. There's a lot of things that you guys are so much more aware of than we were. You're a lot less judgmental than we were. I think you have a lot less hang ups than we did. I think your generation, I'm not knocking them at all. They are just different.

S: Have you ever thought about becoming a politician one day, since you actively participated in those protests?

B: No, I think you have to have a certain type of soul to be a politician. I don't want any part of it. I don't want to play a game where you have to please certain people, you have to please them. I don't like it.

I'll give you an example. We had a woman come in to our charity in May, and she just shot up the door, and I explained to her how we can take you in this time. But you have to email ahead because there's a pandemic going on. We have to space people out. She said, okay, so we let her in. She showed up a month later again, same thing. I said, listen, you have to email us ahead. We have a pandemic; we have to keep people safe. She goes, can I get a call? And I said not right now, because we can't answer the phones because we got five people using the phone currently, so please email us so we can call you back. And for some reason she wrote this horrible Google review, but what a mean guy I am and how I'm not charitable. So the web master called me and said, you got this horrible review, blah, blah, blah. And she goes, I wrote something and she showed it to me, then I found out that she was apologizing to the woman. I said, no, no, we're not apologizing to her. We're doing her no good if we apologize to her. I said she was in the wrong. A politician plays the game, but I like being more straightforward. So the apology didn't go out. There's no way. So I like being straightforward. I can't play that game because it's bullshit. Do I have my views on politics? Absolutely. Are mine necessarily the right ones? No.

S: Last time you mentioned that your best friend had committed suicide when he was in high school, could you provide us with more detail?

B: Doug, he commits suicide, I think at January at 1981. Back then I would be 18 or 19. I don't know why he has chosen to do that. On that day I left him 1/2 an hour before he did it. Okay, see you I'm in half an hour. He did it 1/2 an hour. After he left me, we'd gone downtown or something for the day. And all of a sudden, my sister called me up and said Doug commit suicide and it happened so rapidly that I didn't know who to react to it. I don't think Doug had the childhood and the parenting that children should get, and I think it affects everybody differently. I think it affected Doug very deeply. Doug was a very sensitive guy. And by the way he was a great artist, he painted so beautifully, he drew beautifully. He applied to get into art college. He got turned down. We found out 3 weeks after he killed himself. He wasn't turned down, they sent the wrong letter. He actually got in. I think that has something to do with it, too. It was all a mistake.

S: So he thought he got rejected but in fact he didn't?

B: They hadn't, but they had; they screwed up. The college made a mistake. He was in, but they sent the wrong letter out or something to that effect. Anyways, I think that had something to do with it, but he was a very sensitive guy. And I can't wrap my head around it. And I still can't make sense of it, maybe, because I was too close to it.

S: Yeah. And can you just further describe his personality?

B: It's funny. The way I've met Doug, I was in grade ten. I remembered it like yesterday. We were in class, so he came into English class and I was sitting in his chair. He said, "you're sitting in my chair" and I said," Oh well". he said "get out of my chair", I said, piss off, blah, blah, blah. And he says after school we'll fight. Then I replied let's do it. We go outside after school. I'm ready to fight them. And he goes, "can I borrow a cigarette?" And I was kind of shocked by that? What do you mean? borrow a cigarette? We're supposed to be fighting right now. And he just replied, "well why don't we have a cigarette first? "I said, "Sure". And he goes "well fighting is kind of stupid, and I agreed. So that's the type of guy he was, he was never intended to fight. He probably didn't want to fight; I remember another time. Someone named Lee, who had lived with us at the time, called me a pimple puss because

I had pimples on my face, and Doug just freaked on him. That's the kind of guy who was kind of protective of my feelings, because he was a sensitive guy. I always wonder what would happen if Doug had lived in the relationship we would have had, because we were very close. He lived with us. To this day, I don't know how it(the suicide) affected me. I don't think I ever mourned it, it's like I'm numb to whatever happened that time, it's not something an 18-year-old should go through.

S: That's quite kind of a random question. Sure. Are there a lot of Irish people in Canada (Bill is Irish)?

B: Yes, when I was a kid there were a lot of Irish and a lot of Italians in Canada. Absolutely.

S: Is there a special connection that continuously brings more Irish people to Canada?

B: No, it was desperation; Ireland was very poor. Now, I don't know a lot about it. I've been there. But it wasn't my generation that came. I think it was 2 generations before me. But I have a strong connection to it because. Again, the Irish retreated very badly from the English. They needed to get out of Ireland. There's a lot of poverty and there's a lot of fighting. I was in Northern Ireland during the fighting and you were aware of it.

S: Why do you think that more Irish people are coming into Canada nowadays?

B: Not as much anymore. It was back. Then there were a lot more troubles then compared to right now. There's no more fighting that's over there. But back when I was young, there was a lot of fighting. But I'm just very much a Canadian. I was born here, very much Canadian, but I've always been sort of proud of my Irish roots.

S: After the Irish people came into Canada, did they form their own exclusive community?

B: No, funny enough. The Irish did not do that. There's Irish clubs and stuff like that, but the Irish very much integrated into the melting pot as it were. There's not an Irish town, there's a Greek town, there's Chinatown, but there's not an Irish town, and there's a lot of Irish here. When I go to Ireland, people know I'm Irish, I look at the color of my skin, how white it is, I'm Irish. Background. But I'm a very proud Canadian. I'm more Canadian than American, right? But I have a connection with my Irish roots, because when I was a kid, my grandmother talked a lot about our history.

S: Why do you think the Irish adapted so quickly after they immigrated?

B: I think it's because many Irish came over at the same time, and they just sort of changed the entire foundation of Canadians. That's why I think it probably would have been easier for Irish people to live in Canada.

S: When you first started doing charity in 2007, did you ever think that you would do this for the rest of your life?

B: No, I thought I would do it part-time to get back to the community. In my years of social work, there are certain things I thought affected people more and that's why I started the program. However, I didn't think I would do this for the long term. At the start, I didn't really have any salary but my wife supported me a lot to get to this stage.

S: There any unforgettable stories when you first started this charity?

B: I don't know about unforgettable. I'll tell you why. I'm so immersed in it that sometimes it just takes on, it's like a wheel going faster and faster down a hill. You're just so wrapped up in that wheel, there was not much time to sit and reflect.

There's been some very difficult times where I didn't know if we would be able to stay open, because we didn't have funding. A lot of it seems to be very flowing. A lot of it was a struggle at first; some of it was a struggle to keep going for sure. What I'm now, I started in 2007. Maybe I've done all I can do. You know what I mean like, maybe I'm getting to that point where we've had 4,800 families that are registered here. We've helped a lot of people.

I notice more and more. Other people are doing other things and taking on a bigger role where once it was just me, and I realize that I have to surround myself with people who are experts in certain things that I'm not. I know my limitations. It's amazing and charity work. How much ego is involved? I remember I heard a story. When we first opened, I went to different charities and said, this is who we are. If any of your families need our help, this is what we do.

I remember a staff member of one of the places I went to see their executive director and she told me about a month after I left. The executive director said there's a guy who just wants to be me. Like, I want to be him. There's a lot of ego involved in some of the charities of competition. I would say it's 50 % struggle through the years, and 50 % achievement, I think we've achieved a lot. If I look back on it. I think we've achieved a lot. But it's not the same for me when I first started. I don't look back on and think, did I accomplish great things in blah, blah? I don't have that anymore. It's weird, it's weird. I don't know. If the more I meditate, that's why the mints going into my eyes hurt, the more I meditate, the more you grow, that stuff becomes a little less meaningful. You know what I mean? I don't sit back and think it was great. Even when I got that award, I forgot what it was called; it really wasn't that important to me and? I know people mean well, it just doesn't matter to me as much anymore. I think what really matters to me more now is personal growth. You know what I mean? It's it's. Yeah. Yeah, I think that's more important to me now. The most I enjoy, my time is spending it with my family now, and I'm not as intent on my careers. I once was I think when you're young, that's you know and. You're intent on your career and. You want to get places and you want to accomplish blah, blah, blah. That's funny. It's becoming less important to me.

And I think my first son probably didn't have enough of me as they should have where Riley and Billy got so much more of me because that is more. I see now as important as his family, as once I saw career as an important thing. This is great, it's running well and I still like coming into work. I'd rather work with people more. I don't as much as I used to, because you got to run the place, right? You gotta do the banking, you gotta be meeting with people constantly. I don't work with people as much as I used to. And that was my favorite part, because I enjoyed working with people. Yeah. So I think my intentions have changed.

S: When was your toughest time running this charity?

B: It was at the start throughout the first 4 or 5 years. Like my wife's family said they would help out in that. And then they sort of right to start back down. It's like, so I'm running the place, right? It was very hard to get out there and to get people involved. I remember we have these little boxes to raise money. and I remember this one place, called Geo-tab, who's a very big supporter of us. Then, a woman named Lindy and her mother, Jill, walked into this place and everybody had turned us down with these boxes. I walked in, I said, listen, can we put one of these honor boxes, chocolate boxes in your place? They said," Tell us more about your charity." So I then told them what we do and later they became very involved in SafetyNet.

So you just don't know when you're gonna run into the right people who may show interest. The first five years and that was a struggle. I wasn't getting paid. I think 5 or 6 years, 7 years, my wife did. I had some savings. My wife paid a lot of bills, and it was very difficult. So um I remember 4 years ago and we lost our place down on Randall street. When that guy bought it, he was going to raise the rents 3 times, so we had to leave. It was very hard to find a place. And I didn't know if we were going to. They took about 5 months to find another place, so I thought the charity was done then. But the guy bought the place and it's his right to raise the rent. What are you gonna do?

S: How do your wife help you to operate SaftyNet?

B: She sacrificed a lot. There's times when charity comes first before anything. There's a lot of times we went without pay. We didn't have the money. It was a struggle. She put up a lot for sure. Absolutely. She helped me out when I needed it. Always did. I would say, can you go pick this up for me? And she would go do it. I remember. When we first started, we were doing a bowling tournament. And she went in to raise money and she went into places and asked them a lot. So she's always been a rock for me. Still to this day. She's been the biggest support I've had. A lot of people would say, if your charity, forget it, she didn't. Never been a question of that, never been a question of her support. couldn't have done it without her help, there is just no way, wouldn't have happened.

S: Where do you get all the funding for running this charity?

B: It's a lot of granters, but a lot of dudes come in and do work for us. Chris built the furniture part of it. He made sure that we got enough from the housing department of the region to cover our bills, for guys to be able to take the furniture and pay for the beds and that. Currently, our clothing recycling is doing very well. Then, as I said, there's been some funders and some foundations who have been very helpful. And there were a lot of people who privately helped. I know the people from Geotab have been amazing to us. They've been with me now for 8 years at the support of this charity; they were great to us.

You just gotta get someone to believe in what you're doing. You make enemies along the way, too. You make people get into it for different reasons. There's some people who will turn on you, and that's happened too, like there's some people who get into it for their own egotistical reasons or get into it for their own reasons. And there's times you make some enemies over too, for sure. There's some times that there's been conflict.

S: Are you comfortable sharing with us how exactly they applied harmful things to this charity?

B: So there was one woman who wanted to be on the board, and I had nothing to do with it. But she wanted to be on the board and she had already done a fundraiser first, the board at the time said that they wanted her to volunteer a bit longer, and had nothing to do with me. She got so angry that they didn't accept her as one of the Board members. And for some reason, she turned on me. She started bad multimedia in the community. Had nothing to do with me. But it's like, all three of us can look at that table and come up with a very different perspective of what it is that we see. What you have to understand is that people have very different perspectives on life, you are and people don't see things as they are, they see things as what they think they are. If you have somebody who's got a certain way of seeing things, there's no pleasing them, and you gotta learn that. Yeah, it's very hard because you're protecting of the charity. There's times I take things very much to heart..

S: When you first started the charity, SafteyNet, in 2007, you first thought that it would just be more like a part time job.

B: Yeah, I did.

S: What are the reasons that pushed you to turn it into a lifelong career?

B: There are 2 things that pushed me to do that: the need in the community and my own ego. Two things simple as that. At that time almost everyone told me that my charity is not going to survive and I was told it would never happen. I was going to prove people that they are wrong, that's maybe not the best way to do things, but that's the truth.

Furthermore, there was a lot of need at the time. The people started getting busier and busier. It was those two things. Do I love helping people? Absolutely. That was part of the motivation 100 %, but the other part that I'm gonna be totally honest, it was partly ego too, because I was told it couldn't be accomplished. And so I said to them, "watch me." There's two things and just don't get me wrong. There's part of me that really genuinely wants to help people. And that was a huge motivating factor in the start of it. Yeah. But then other things started happening, too. And so the eagle became a part of it as well. I am not a saint.

During the pandemic. Lee, who I think I may have talked about. Yes, when I was growing up, he died. Yeah, he died. He left me his Mercedes Benz, which is very kind of him. And he tried to help me out and he tried to pay me back, he left $50,000 for my kids when they go to school.

And Lee, I think I talked quite a bit about that. I talked much about Lee growing up. He was in my house. He was my sister's boyfriend when she got pregnant and he lived with us. Back then I had a lot of fear of Lee because Lee didn't have the childhood he should have, and he could be violent at times. But the last few years we connected again, and he was very good to me, he never forgot our old times. He died last August. Again, I don't know how to really, I don't think I've come to understand how it affected me, just like the time when Doug died. And it was very sad. So I went to his funeral and there weren't a lot of people there because it was during a pandemic. And he was very good to us. He really tried to help when he died because he made a lot of money. He became very good and self educated at stocks. He did very well. He really took care of my family, and it was very much appreciative. I think with Lee, we had a very close connection growing up. When we were young, there was a lot of fear, but then, as I got older and became a boxer and stuff like that, we became more equal terms and became closer. We had a time where we fell apart a bit, but in the last 3 or 4 years of his life, he called me up and said I'd like to reconnect. And I said, yeah, okay. And uh and he did a lot for my family, like as I said, he left things for my kid's future, which is very kind of them. Yeah, MHM.

S: What is the group of people that has the most demand for SafteyNet's clothing?

B: Right now, it's refugees for sure that's what we're seeing the most while helping people. I would say new Canadians in general have high demand on clothing.

S: How many families have you helped last year?

B: I think probably I would say 1200 to 1,500 families easily. I could get you the statistics right away, but I would say, I thought in my head probably that, yeah, new Canadians who come here and they need help. Yeah.

S: Has it always been the case that newcomers are the ones needing help from SafetyNet the most?

B: No, absolutely not. At first, it was a lot of people who were single mothers, people experiencing financial difficulties. It was the last during the Syrian crisis that we saw a lot of families who are refugees that we helped out. It's okay. In fact, we've had Spanish in Arabic interpreters working with us the last 3 years. All right.

S: Do you think that the government is doing enough to help those newcomers who just came to Canada?

B: Yeah, I think you did. I really do. I think you can point your fingers at the liberals for this and that. However, I think Canada did very well with the refugees. Canada did the best in the world, Canadians are very compassionate, when Trump said, no, we're not taking any of them in. Canada said we're gonna help, which I think they do. Do I always love the government? No, but do I think it's a good job for refugees? Yes. And I think Canadian people in general are compassionate, the politicians represent the people's views. So let's call out what it is. Canadians are a little more compassionate than most, a little more welcoming.

I think in the states right now, there's a lot of racism, having to do with the Chinese community. I don't think you see that as much in Canada. Now I could be wrong, it may be happening. I'm sure it could be. But nothing to the degree of what we're seeing down. I think we're a little less flag waving, and I think we're a little less prejudiced. I think we're a little more welcoming of people. I think we are much more open. I think we were a little more for the underdog. We're educated.

S: Compared to other cities in Ontario, is the number of charities in Oakville above average or below average?
B: I think we meet the needs. It's just we meet the needs. Toronto has a lot more charities. They have a lot more needs because it has a higher population. I find Toronto more charitable than Oakville for sure. That's gonna get me in trouble, but I do, I find people a little more sensitive in Toronto as far as helping. I worked in both. I did a lot of work.

S: Why do you think that education is a key to break the closed loop of poverty?

B: Two things. Education gives you a better chance of the job and it opens your mind. Life experience in education opens your mind. I remember. The first time in college, I heard about feminism, I said, yeah, for sure. First time I opened a book about Buddhism or opened a book about different philosophies and. I first read Descartes or Nietzsche or the first time I heard the Beatles sing, all you need is love. I just educate and being exposed to things, open your mind and I think education. It's not only good for a job. It just makes you a more open and well-rounded person. Education, I think it's very practical to get someone out of poverty. And it's also good for self-growth.

S: How much money do you need to pay for running the facility?

B: Right here including the taxes right now is $6,900 a month. The other place, including taxes is $3,400 a month.

S: That's quite expensive.

B: It's Oakville, the richest city in Canada, you're not getting anything for Free.

S: Are you paying the rent yourself or do you get a lot of funds?

B: We get funds, we raise money. It's mostly what we raise though the furniture and the clothing absolutely.

S: How many people are using the new department right now

B: No one yet. But we hope to have 50 kids being tutored there. Yes, we hope to have that many this year, I think at the end of last year um, I think we had 42, I believe.

S: Are you satisfied with your current living condition?

B: Yeah. Absolutely.

S: Yes. I don't know. How did you Guide your children during their time?

B: I think the key is listening to them, I just listened to him. Yeah, absolutely. Listen. And be there. And the biggest thing you can do for a child is to listen to them. The most important thing is, there's no proper way to raise a child because every child is different, you have to understand who the child is in their own personality. I think the best thing to do generally is to just be there and accompany them; be there to spend time, listen and spend time. It doesn't have to be obligatory. It doesn't have to be an obligation like, but you can spend time listening and be there for them. Absolutely. The biggest thing, though, is finding out what's important to them and spending time with that. Yeah.

S: Was there any organization you looked up to when you first started Safetynet? Were there any people supporting you when you started?

B: No, I was alone when I started this organization. I have this idea on my own, for the first few years, I ran this organization on my own. My mother-in-law even said no one is going to need items of clothing, turns out to be that she's wrong. Over the years I gathered many volunteers and people added to the charity. Over the years, people gave me a lot of support. However, some people get involved in the charity for some self-centered reasons, they take away from the charity; there are some negative people in the world. I try to surround myself with experts because I don't know everything, having them is my pleasure. They helped me.

S: Why did you start the charity in a wealthy town like Oakville? Would you help more people if you started in a not so wealthy town?

B: No, I started in Oakville because of the perception that Oakville is the land of milk and honey and people thought there were no problems here. I know that there are problems. people are not willing to ask for help in such an environment and that's why I started the program here. Plus, it was my community and I want to get back to it. We are up to 4200 families in service and it turns out that people still need help in Oakville. That being said, we also assisted people in other areas such as Hamilton, however, our major focus is still in the Halton region.

S: The charity work you are doing right is supposed to be the government's job. In your opinion, what did the Canadian government do well on in the case of helping the vulnerable group and what did they need to improve on?

B: Canada has a sort of social safety net, so a lot of people that we work with have disabilities for people who can't work. but to be frank with you, people with disabilities, they can't afford things like clothing, dishes and furniture. That's when we came in.

As well they can't afford some of the basics for their children like torturing. And the way to break the cycle of poverty is to offer the child education. Chances are that those parents didn't have a chance to receive college-level education, and that's why offering tutoring makes so much sense. Parents with minimum wage can't support their children's hobbies. That's why my program is having things like music classes. For the children who have talent, money should not be a barrier for them.

S: How much do you need to pay for all of these?

B: It seems that you are very concerned about whether I can have enough money to run this charity organization, thank you. Like I just said, with clean taxes, we are paying 6900 dollars per month for renting the place, and about 2000 dollars for utilities. we're probably between 8500 to 9000 dollars a month for the facility. We have several places to donate to the charities. Our biggest donation gives us 2000 dollars quarterly. When I started the charity I tried to make it sufficient, we have a recycling system for the clothing we can't use, we get money for that.

S: While you are running Safetynet, where does your salary come from?

B: My salary I would say comes from people who donate money to the charity and it comes from furniture apartment reimbursement as well as clothing reimbursement. We never really got a grant for my salary, however we just got to Grants to hire summer students. We also got a grant to hire one more person until March to work in the furniture Bank because the furniture was pretty busy right now due to this virus outbreak.

S: Do your children like charity? Are they proud of what you are doing? Do you want them to follow your footsteps?

B: My youngest enjoys going to charity. I do think my children support me for raising this charity. And no, I don't have any aspirations for what they are going to do in the future, I don't want them to simply follow in my footsteps, I want them to live their own life.

S: Do all the clothing need to be disinfected before donated?

B: Every cloth donated needs to be washed before being donated, but I would say 60% of the clothing we get is not washed. but those clothes still help the charity since we can recycle it. We don't put stuff out unless it's clean, in good shape and fairly modern because I want people to come in and get nice clothing. I think that's important.

S: Does the government have a standard on the clothing to be donated?

B: No, there's no government standard on clothing. We do all the standard. Our standards are very high, mainly because I make them high. People like to give to us because we give clothing for free.

S: When you are donating the clothing, how do you hand them out?

B: We let the families who are below the poverty line pick their clothing. They are allowed to come in quarterly, the family law to give four shirts, four pants, one pair of shoes, two shirts, two dresses, one coat, one pair of shoes and soft underwear per member. Right now we can only let one person enter at a time.

S: Does furniture need to be disinfected before donated?

B: We have three volunteers to fix the furniture. We don't hand out broken ones to them.

S: Is there expensive, very expensive furniture received?

B: Yes, some people donate us some nice furniture. We also sell the ones we can't use, however, we don't get a lot of refund from this.

S: Would you ever directly give money to families?

B: No, we are not allowed to do that. We hand out gift cards to children sometimes. But we can't give out money.

S: How do you give out big furniture?

B: When delivering big furniture, the Ontario government needs to approve the delivery. Once the family is approved by the government, we can then deliver the item to them.

S: Could you tell us the exact numbers of the items you donated?

B: In 2019, we donated 1,240,021 pieces in total. We gave out 32,234 diapers, 5794 pairs of pants, 2498 pieces of furniture, 7500 shirts, 163 bikes, and 2608 pieces of houseware. Until now we serviced 4203 families and 810 refugee families.

S: If someone rides your bike and gets into an accident, do you need to take responsibility for it?

B: No, not at all. when they receive the bike, it is their responsibility. We don't give out sensitive items that too many people recall.

S: Do you have a legal adviser?

B: Yes, we have a lawyer that we can access, I never really used him though. Technology can do almost everything now.

S: In the 14 years that you opened Safetynet, did you ever think about quitting?

B: No, one time I had a few very egotistical board members and I didn't enjoy working with them. But I never thought about quitting.

S: Has your charity ever encountered a situation that needs to be closed down?

B: It happened a few times, there was a time when we didn't have enough money. Another time is when I can't afford the rent. The other time is when there are not enough resources.

S: Would you consider this pandemic a big challenge for the charity? How much of an impact did it bring?

B: It's a challenge not for the charity, but for me. It was very hard for me to operate on my own, I had quite an anxiety during this virus outbreak. I felt like I was being exposed even though I followed the social distance. The last three month were hard for me.

S: How did the family get affected by this outbreak?
B: The number all went up a bit because many lost their jobs. We haven't been able to serve many families because we can only serve one at a time. There's a lot of people who are suffering psychologically. People are suggging and we are aware of that.

S: Would the City Hall of Oakville support you? Do they give you any bonus when you are doing well?
B: Not really, I see them at meetings but other than that, we don't have contact with each other. We are sort of on our own. But a lot of people support us.

S: Should the government give any help to the charity?
B: I mean there's not much they can do right now. They are pretty stressed too right now.

S: Does the government inspect the charity?

B: No, we are aware of what needs to happen.

S: Does your charity need advertising?

B: We have two people working on our social media but we don't spend any money on advertising.

S: Are the previous donors loyal to the charity?

B: There's some expectation, however, most people are constantly donating. The donors are pretty loyal to us.

S: Do you have any competitors? If so, what areas are you competing in?

B: There's not a competition going on, other charities might not work and cooperate with us for various reasons, but there's not much for us to compete for.

S: Is there anyone who debates the charity on the website?

B: Not on the website, on the website it's all five stars rating. However, there is someone who decided not to like us, and there's not much I can do.

S: How does your board of directors' work?

B: We gather talented people and make them do good work with their talent. I don't want people to just advise me, I want them to get their hands dirty and fully use their talent.

S: What advice would you give to someone who's starting a charity like SafetyNet?

B: First of all, it's going to be a struggle for the first little while. Surround you with people who can contribute to the charity who have a certain talent who can help out. But the main point is to have a passion and belief in what you are doing. You need to develop a program that can assist people.

And again it takes time to learn certain things and become an expert at it, but you can't just simply surround yourself with experts, you need to work your way there. But the biggest thing is to have a passion for what you are doing.

S: Did the charity receive more donations of clothing during the pandemic?

B: Yeah, we did very well.

S: Are there any individuals or families that you helped previously who later became an active volunteer to this charity?

B: A couple, not a lot, and to be honest, with a couple of times we did, it didn't work out so well.

S: What's the reason?

B: I think they just have too many other struggles to really be focused on the charity aspect of it. I did it a couple of times. And it didn't work out well. Now that being said, no, I shouldn't say that because the two guys that work for me first came here using the charity and eventually hired them. And that worked out very well. So that's not true. We hired the guys who came here. They showed up needing help, and they were refugees, and they're doing very well working now. So that's yeah.

S: What kind of furniture is the most needed?

B: Right now? Couches and tables and chairs are the big things always. The practical stuff.

S: How was your board of directors established?

B: People, a lot more volunteers here. Like Brian, who's up front right now. She was a volunteer here and a number of them volunteer here first. And then they became interested in having a bigger role. So a lot of more volunteers at one time that's.

S: When was it first formed?

B: First, as people I ask for help. That was the first. And then over time people have been volunteering here, and they have different specialties. And so we access them in the board and that capacity of their specialties. For example, we have a person named Bran who does human resources. She has a human resources background. She advises young human resources. Katrina was a volunteer here who is in the bank and. She does a lot of the treasurer for us.

S: Have they ever caused you any trouble?

B: We've had a few that have the eagles and they were pain in the ass.

S: How could you just sort of elaborate on this?

B: I remember one who I had a disagreement with who said I was just disagreeing with her because she's a woman. I was raised with just women. No, I disagree with something you're doing. And their way it had to be their way. It had to be this way and it's definitely wrong. To the day stuff the board has really no say over it's I run the charity. But we've had some dudes come in and said this is the way it should be. We've never really stepped inside the charity. And so. They don't know. For some reason, they have to try to search for some authority and it doesn't make sense. There's been times with a few of them. I really bank heads absolutely. They're kind of sticking their nose where it shouldn't be.

S: They are just making criticism out of nowhere.

B: Yes, absolutely. And it was difficult. There's a time for a couple of years that we had a board that was really, extremely hard to work with. I almost left the charity.

S: Which part of the charity is the most important? Is it like the financial part? Or human resource management.

B: The most important program I think we run is tutoring. Because it leads out. The most important thing we need is always money. You cannot run without it. The size we are now. You need the money.

S: Last time you mentioned that the charity also almost closed down due to financial issues. Could you just expand that story and tell us a little more?

B: It was time we couldn't make rent. And luckily at the time, the landlord then was a little more understanding. He let things go. But there's times, there were a few times, in the first few years, we couldn't make rent, we didn't have enough money for rent. And he was a little more understanding and he gave me some breaks and we were lucky, but I came close to closing down because we couldn't make it to the end. We just didn't have the money come in. We were well known yet.

S: Do you think that charities in Oakville are now stabilized, or do they need more help from the government?

B: It's stabilized. But growing up, the way I did with lack of resources and lack of money, I always have a parent way that we're going to run. But for me, for this charity, I can't speak for other charities. But for me, the way I grew up with lack of money, always and lack of resources. There's always that part of me who's always worried about it.

S: Yeah, for sure. Has any other sort of public media, such as newspaper, radio and TV programs that publicize you and your charity.

B: Not in Oakville, the media is horrible out here. We have the beaver. It's awful, right? And they have their favorites, but I don't like the media, like Facebook has done well to bring awareness. But I don't want media for what we do. And I'll tell you why, because you get these people who go down the street in the hand, a sandwich to a poor person, a homeless person and he filmed the whole thing. It's terrible. Like, who are you doing it for them? You're doing it for yourself, you're doing it for your own. Look how good I am. I don't like and I don't like that aspect of it. I really don't like there was some group who was doing a thing for homeless people and they're taking pictures of the homeless people well. The reason why you don't if you're gonna give to somebody just do it without the fanfare, do it without talking about it. Is the media supporting Oakville? No, not really, no.

S: And how's your social media accounts for this charity?

B: Very good. They're doing very well. We have a woman named Ali who runs it and she does a very good job. Mostly Facebook and Instagram, I believe. Yeah. But you're dealing with the public, which is not always the easiest thing, too, right? So right.

Chapter three

"Keep your distance from the grantee"

——Interview with Bill's friend, senior charity participant Wen Yang

By Zhaoyan Sun and Zhaohan Sun

Sun(S):　　You have always been very enthusiastic to help low-income people, and often do charity. When did you get used to doing charity?

Wen Yang(Y): Charity is just my hobby, it only takes up a small part of my time and energy. I am a registered accountant. My current company is an accounting firm. The company will initiate diversified charitable activities-larger companies in Canada, as long as they are not independent individual companies, will generally organize similar charitable activities on a regular basis. There is a goal each year, mainly to achieve the established donation amount in the future. Donations vary from year to year. For one hundred dollars, the company will donate another fifty dollars.

In addition, others will make clothes for events and activities that occur during company events.

We are an accounting company, and Canadians also need to submit their own annual tax returns. If they have trouble filing their own taxes, we provide tax filing services for free. This allows us to use our unique resources for social charity activities.

S: Canadians have a clear understanding of charity. There are many types of charity, not just donating money and materials, like your company, which obliges residents to file tax returns. This kind of charity is more precious to those who need it, and it can solve their urgent needs. How many employees participated in the charity activities organized by your company?

Y:　Estimated to be less than 5%. The company will not participate in organized activities, but will participate in other types of charitable activities. The activities organized by the company are organized activities. The company has different types of activities every year. Activities attended by different people may not participate next year. . All this is changing.

S: Did your company's charitable activities this year, the organization they donated to meet your wishes? If it doesn't, do you have a choice? Can you refuse?

Y: I personally can choose. The company's activities this year are not bad, and I agree with it. It seems that last year, changes have taken place. Yes, if I participate together, it doesn't matter. Taking advantage of the seriousness of the epidemic, I didn't have it myself.

For example, the company encourages employees to do community service. You can organize community activities or directly participate in community activities. As long as you complete 30 hours of community service, the company can quote it, and the company will give you money for the entire community. .

S: Listening to your introduction, your company is very charitable and has a sense of serving the society. Is Canada as active as your company in philanthropy? Do they have similar charity activities?

Y: I don't know the specific data, but based on my instinct, I think Canadian companies are the most important. Generally, they actively participate in charitable activities because it has something to do with the model. Another good mechanism for Canadian companies to do charity is social responsibility. From the perspective of the whole society, everyone is a citizen. The responsibility of social citizens should be the responsibility of every enterprise. So generally speaking, every company will take charity as a daily work, as a choice in business, to provide support.

Of course, if the company is too small, such as a one-person company or a family company, if there is no cost and the scale of operation is small, it will be more difficult for them to do charity.

S: I understand. The company's philanthropy, in addition to the boss's kindness, and transcendence, the main driving force comes from the system design. Taxation encourages companies to do more charity. Another driving force is the company's awareness of citizenship or social responsibility. This sense of social responsibility depends on the nostrils.

Y: Yes, the company's civic awareness also has a process of mutual influence and even competition. It seems that other companies have to do like ours. Other brands and my image, such as other companies, are not as fresh and charming as my own. So positive. Think about it, it can help community residents, especially low-income families, file tax returns. Everyone's donation method is different. I think it is a more effective way to do charity by providing free services. The more developed the society, the more professional service classification, coupled with complexity and high prices.

S: In addition to compulsory tax filing, there are also legal services. Lawyers can provide free lawyer services for charity; there are psychological consultations, children's education and parent-child relationship adjustment, and pet services. These special services are not all companies providing services on a voluntary basis?

Y: Really, all the professional services you can think of, you can find the corresponding charity company. So you see, doing charity is a very professional and complicated thing, and it's more than just donating money and materials.

Of course, donating money and materials, especially food, must be the most direct and effective charity action. Look at the bread-making companies and biscuits companies in Canada. They will have many activities throughout the year to provide their products, that is free food, to low-income families. Of course, the cost and related expenses of these foods they provide are not entirely borne by the company, and he is tax deductible.

S: Accounting companies provide voluntary tax filing services for low-income groups. Bread companies provide free food. Companies that build airplanes are more troublesome. They cannot give airplanes to the poor.

Y: Haha, yes, it seems that the poor don't need to put a plane in the garage, it is enough if they have a car. But companies that build airplanes can hire more people and make more people employed. Are we going to digress? To develop the aviation industry and increase employment opportunities seems to be an issue that the Prime Minister of Canada should consider.

S: You mentioned earlier that if the charitable activities of the company meet your wishes, you will participate; otherwise, you will not participate. In addition to selectively participating in charitable activities organized by the company, do you also participate in other charitable activities? Would you choose charities outside the company to participate in their activities?

Y: This is a good question. My family and I like to participate in activities organized by non-profit charitable organizations that are truly charitable in nature.

You know, even in Canada, charities are diverse. When I choose a charity, I usually look at its public information first. Such charitable organizations will be registered with the government, and the government will publish their rankings every year. Various indicators are available, especially its operating cost, which accounts for a large proportion of all donated funds and materials. Its public welfare will be weaker-it will use the money donated by others to support its own people, which is not good. Charity organizations in Canada also require annual review.

Of course, the annual review will not be so strict. The annual review report issued is mainly to help ordinary people who participate in charity, so that everyone can choose those who do charity more efficiently and spend more money. Effective institutions. The list of charities and their rankings are updated every year.

S: We finally got to our topic: Why did you choose to help Bill's charity? Is it because his organization is higher in the ranking list that you said is updated every year?

Y : Bill is a legendary figure, and many people in Oakville know him. His charity organization is also very famous, because of the long time, so everyone also trusts him and his organization. We chose him completely because we trust him, and it has little to do with rankings. But I think his organization must be very high in the ranking above.

There are indeed some negative examples. There was a report in the news a few years ago that a charity man who lives in the north of Toronto used charity to make money on a large scale and registered two charities, but he has several sets. Luxury houses, as well as luxury goods such as sports cars and boats, make life very luxurious. He defrauded a lot of money with charity organizations. He also married a 20-year-old wife in Africa. After being reported in the first year, his organization was still included in the list of legal charities in the second year. Later, when people kept reporting him, the police started investigating him. After obtaining the evidence, they started to arrest him; but it seems that they haven't caught him yet.

This is a scandal; do you watch TV? A channel of CBC in Canada often presents this kind of revealing program, revealing it deeply. Every country has a dark and ugly side. Even in a country like Canada, the social supervision system is very sound, and civic awareness is very popular, there will be things that make money under the banner of charity.

Therefore, to do charity in Canada, you must first understand the most basic rules, refer to a lot of relevant information, and have a pair of insights. Otherwise, it is very possible to do bad things with good intentions, spend money, and ultimately fail to help those in need, but instead provide the bad guys with more opportunities to do evil.

S: Shouldn't it be the government's responsibility to supervise charitable organizations?

Y: It is indeed the responsibility of the government. I heard that some institutions have been banned by the government. Of course, in real life, there are not so many bad and fake charities. Most of them are trustworthy like Bill's. This is the essential difference between developed and developing countries. I can also say this: If you don't want to bother to identify the pros and cons of charities, you can do charity based on your own interests and hobbies: if you want to help small animals, you go to such an institution; you want To help the elderly, you can go to the elderly rehabilitation center to volunteer, or donate money and materials.

S: Could it be that many Canadians are reluctant to do charity activities because of the above fake charity scam news?

Y: On the contrary, the people around me and I have strengthened our confidence in doing charity within our power after seeing this news. And this news is a bit like teaching courses. After you read it, you will find out which ones are real charities and which ones are fake ones.

Another point is that we are all ordinary people, and the assets in the family are not so large that they donate tens of thousands and hundreds of thousands every year. The total donation of ordinary families and individuals is between a few hundred and a few thousand. At least it can reach tens of thousands or tens of thousands; if it reaches hundreds of thousands, it must not be ordinary people and ordinary families. So we don't have to worry too much about donating too much, right, just donate money and things, just the volunteer time, just donate and do the right thing.

S: As a donor or volunteer, what rights do you think you have?

Y: The most important right of a donor is that you can choose who you want to donate. After confirming who you donate, you can also choose different ways of donation when possible, and specify how the money or items are used. For example, if you donate money to your school, you can ask the school to use the money only for the purchase of teaching equipment or only for scholarships. You can ask the school not to use the money for the purchase of dolls or for teachers. You have the right to issue year-end bonuses, and so on.

Also, donations and volunteers from ordinary people, for those who are in urgent need of help and families, it is difficult to provide charcoal in a snowy, let alone continuous and persistent. The fundamental social assistance must be the government and organized. A task that can only be accomplished by a charity.

For example, for the relief of homeless people, ordinary people and families cannot provide long-term residences. Only the government and some religious groups have the strength to do such things.

S: When I usually drive, I can find that although there are not many homeless people in Canada, they are not uncommon. Especially in the central area of the city, you can always see homeless people. But I also heard that religious organizations such as the Canadian government and churches are capable of providing the most basic living conditions for these homeless people, but they are accustomed to being homeless and unwilling to go. Is that so?

Y: Yes, it is not like this.

The reason for this is because the Canadian government's social relief force is still very strong. This is mainly because Canada has a small population and abundant social resources. After the outbreak of the new crown epidemic, the Canadian government has issued several rounds of money to all its citizens, which of course also includes these homeless people with Canadian nationality. These homeless people can have basic livelihood security with this money.

The reason why this is not the case is that even in a relatively wealthy country like Canada, in Oakville, which is known as the richest city in Canada, the conditions for housing and shelter for homeless people may not be too good. It's best to just let them live in it, it's impossible for them to live comfortably, eat happily, and have fun.

I know that a shelter run by a political organization provides a place to sleep and bathe for homeless people, and they can also receive meals, but the conditions are really normal. There is no hot water after taking a bath. After a while, there will be no hot water; You need to make an appointment for the place, or you can say it, the first one has a place to sleep, and the later one has no place. The meal should be on time, and it will be gone after a while. To get these subsidies, homeless people have to arrive at any time like they are at work. For some vagrants who are very old, physically disabled, mentally poor, and have insufficient personal capabilities, this is really too difficult.

Therefore, for most people who are accustomed to wandering, they would rather sleep on the streets than squeeze into shelters where conditions are not good or even poor. Over time, they will get used to wandering. But you can't say that they like this kind of wandering life, and you can't stand and talk without backache, saying that they love wandering, which is a bit of taking the pain of others to consume and enjoy. You can only say that this is their last resort.

The government's shelters, with financial support, can only provide some basic shelters without compulsion. Other religious or social organizations are even less expected. Some social relief places are only open two or three days a week. As a person, you can't just eat two days a week or sleep only three days. Therefore, this kind of unsustainable assistance is not very effective for those people and families who have been in trouble and misfortune for many years.

S: Let's go back to your own charity activities. You are the mother of two children. Have your current charity activities changed with the changes in your living conditions than before?

Y: You are too right. After having two lovely babies, I am more willing to help low-income families with children, or directly help the children.

Now that the epidemic is not over, many schools are taking online classes, and schools will have a greater investment in online class equipment. For the school I donated, I set the direction of donation to improve and improve the quality of the school's online courses, let them upgrade the equipment, make the Internet faster, and so on.

For specific people with family difficulties, if my husband and I know about it, we will also directly donate some money and goods through intermediaries to help them. There was a family a while ago. The child suffered from severe depression. He especially liked to ride a bicycle. We donated a bicycle to him through an intermediary.

S: Why did you go through the middleman instead of buying him a bicycle directly?

Y: This is the way we are accustomed to. We are generally unwilling or accustomed to directly facing the rescued object. After all, it's two families. We just want to do as little charity as we can, and we don't want to build too much and too deep personal feelings for the rescued. This will cause a variety of problems and cause a lot of unnecessary trouble for both parties.

Of course, from the perspective of the grantees, they are unwilling to face the donors directly. On the one hand, this will bring psychological reasons for themselves, and on the other hand, for the underage children, they will recognize the gap between the rich and the poor prematurely. Social inequality or inequality will do more harm than good to their physical and mental health.

There is also the Chinese people's habit of repaying gratitude. If the donor and the recipient face each other directly, will they repay the gratitude? How to repay the favor? Do you want to continue donating after repaying your favor? All of these will have unexpected and possibly serious consequences.

S: That's true. In China, we often hear similar stories. Donors and recipients end up being enemies that don't share the same sky.

Y: So to do charity, you have to have a normal heart, just make some contribution to the society within your capacity, don't think about who is grateful, let alone what kind of repayment and feedback you will get.

S: Your story of "donating bicycles" is a good example. It has a clear guiding significance for how to deal with the relationship between donors and recipients. Maybe this is the reason for the existence of institutions like Bill and his.

Y: Yes, in system design, the following two

points should be done:

First of all, it is necessary to remind the donors repeatedly that donation itself is the meaning, it is the honor and the reward; the donors should not think about getting grateful and getting feedback. A mature society, a person with a mature social consciousness, must have a sufficiently open and tolerant attitude to do charity.

Second, in charitable activities, we should also protect the recipients, not let them feel inferior, or ask them to express gratitude to everyone. No matter how developed a country is, there will always be low-income people; no matter how rich a city is, there will always be homeless people; these low-income people, these wandering people, their misfortune, are essentially social development and social operation. The price that must be paid; these costs have unfortunately come to them, and the entire society, including us, who already have more social resources and who have no worries about food and clothing, have an obligation to help them.

There is also a third point. No matter who you are, there is no guarantee that you will not fall into the low-income group in the future, so helping others is helping yourself. You have made a little more contribution to building a more complete charity system in this country and this city, and you have made a little more guaranteeing contribution to yourself and your family.

S: The second point you mentioned is very interesting and important. Don't put pressure on the recipient, especially don't let the underage children feel that their family is being rescued. This is often overlooked.

Y: Canada has done a good job in this regard. For example, in schools, if students come from low-income families, many of their expenses will be waived, but this will only be told to their parents and families. The school will never tell other students and parents, let alone treat them differently..

Of course, the school will perform verification before reducing or exempting these fees, but the verification process is very careful and will not embarrass these families and children. After all, in any country and society, living in poverty and poverty is an unpleasant experience.

In addition, the school also has other benefits specifically for low-income families, but these benefits are voluntary, and the school must first seek the consent of these families before distributing them; at the same time, the disbursement process is also back to back, and each other is mutually exclusive. Don't understand. This protects the dignity of low-income families to the greatest extent and protects the innocence of children from harm.

S: Are all your charitable activities conducted through intermediaries?

Y: It's basically like this.

Here is another example. A while ago, my father was ill and was hospitalized. After the operation, I bought him a lot of food. A patient on his wall saw the pile of food on the bedside of my father's bed and he was too hungry. Obviously he wanted to eat these things too. Lives very far, and it takes three hours to go back and forth from his house to the ward. Seeing his desire, I gave him something to eat. He was very happy and told me that he is a music teacher who teaches some very special children to learn music. Among these children are patients with cerebral palsy and brain damage. There are patients with depression, and other disabled children.

In addition to these disabled children, there are some children who seem normal and healthy, but their families have problems, mainly because both or one of the parents take drugs, and the children are unattended.

After I listened to his story, I treated him as a middleman. I used him to provide disabled children and children from drug addicts with some items to help them.

S: Parents take drugs and children suffer.

Y: It's like this. In the eyes of Chinese people, drug users are bad guys; but in reality, the situation is very complicated. There is a drug-addicted mother. She is a single mother and she has to go out to work. The child's living environment is complicated and difficult. Her child cannot get help from other people because of her mother's drug abuse, right.

We must treat everyone equally, but life itself is unequal. For children, the environment they face is very different after they are born. The work of this music teacher is actually half a charity event; of course he also makes a living from it. I think it is very appropriate for him to be my charity intermediary.

S: Let's be one building first. Are there many drug users in Canada? What do they do because of drug abuse?

Y: There are too many reasons for taking drugs, and they are too complicated. It is impossible to say that taking drugs is a bad person. I personally think that it is mainly due to the influence of the family environment. If parents take drugs, the possibility of children taking drugs will greatly increase. This also reminds us that we should pay more attention to the children of drug users.

Of course, there are also some high-income families who have raised a lot of worthless children. In addition to parents, there are social influences, as well as relatives and friends.

I think most of the inequality of people is acquired. Children from low-income families are more likely to take drugs. Parents usually work late and don't have time to accompany their children, and their children will be more affected by society. For example, for myself, my focus is on what clothes to wear in the morning to go to school; many children with problems in the family, they do not even care about their breakfast, although there is no shortage of food, but what to eat and what to wear, all have to be small children If you decide for yourself, it's easy to make misjudgments, and it's easy to be affected by social factors prematurely. So in Canada, many of the motives of drug users are beyond the control of individuals.

S: Let's go back to the topic again. What kind

of things do you generally donate to others?

Y: There is no definite rule. For example, after I gave birth to my second treasure, my mother-in-law bought me a very expensive and advanced breast pump, worth about 500 Canadian dollars. But just in time for the epidemic, I was working at home, and I could breastfeed at home, so I didn't need this maternal suction device. Through a charity intermediary, I gave this very expensive and of course very useful breast pump to another young single mother who needed it.

Of course, more often it is to give money and use money to buy. Once, I saw on Facebook that a family needed a mattress, so I suggested to the middleman that I could pay the money, ask the middleman to help, buy them a mattress, and send it to their home. I prefer this approach. The money is not spent in vain and it solves the specific difficulties of a certain person.

S: Listening to your introduction, you have helped many people. Do you have someone to help? How many years have you been helping someone?

Y: It doesn't seem to be. My husband and I help people at random. Others are others, and we are us. Once we know who needs help, we will help him in our own way. Once we help, we will end. There is no continuous connection and extra emotions between each other.

Of course, there are people who are helped who want to contact us. There is a little girl, because I always buy kimonos for her, and I gave her a lot of gifts at Christmas. She went through the middle teacher and said that she wanted to get to know me. I just thought, I just gave her some gifts, but I am not her teacher, I have no obligation to educate and enlighten her, and of course I don't have the motivation to establish intimate relationships with such a small girl. Another reason is, I was too busy to spare time to chat with this little girl, so I declined her request through the teacher.

S: You are a very rational person. Keeping a distance is more difficult than establishing contact. Does your husband support you in doing this?

Y: He is too supportive. He is also very enthusiastic about charity, but he is more rational. What he cares most about is the efficiency of our work, in other words, whether we can really help the people we want to help.

S: I asked a question that may involve privacy. If you think it is inappropriate, you can refuse to answer-how much money does your family spend on charity and helping others each year? Specifically last year, how much did you spend?

Y: This is not privacy, I can answer. Last year, we just filed a tax return, and the money spent on charitable activities last year was more than 1,000 Canadian dollars.

S: That's a lot.

Y: But we also often directly buy some things and donate them. The money is not included in the 1,000 Canadian dollars; there are also some second-hand old items, we have not calculated the value, such as the breast pump just mentioned, the original price five hundred Canadian dollars, but we will not count it as a cash donation. If these things are not handed over to people to use, they will not be worth a penny. They must be used by people in order to be valuable.

As for daily shopping and giving away, things like this always happen randomly. For example, the music teacher I just mentioned, sometimes we go to Toronto, and when we think about it, we buy a bunch of food and send it there. We don't deliberately count the money.

S: What kind of food do you usually buy for them?

Y: Mainly it is some necessities of life, but also the kind that can be stored for a long time. Things like spaghetti and canned food.

S: It's a bit like during Chinese New Year holidays, grassroots government officials give rice, flour and oil to poor households. This is called "sending warmth" in China. Whoever receives these things feels warm and warm.

Y: That's true, but when you buy food in Canada to give to others, you must be very careful. We usually only send to those who are particularly familiar with and understand.

First of all, you need to understand whether this person has religious and cultural taboos in eating. Canada is a diversified society and adopts an attitude of tolerance and respect for various religions and cultures. Different religions have different food taboos. This requires Before you give food to others, do your homework in this respect so as not to offend the other person.

Second, in Canada, we must attach great importance to food allergies. The entire society attaches great importance to this issue, and the school reminds students every day: Do not bring food containing peanuts and other nuts to the school, because similar tragedies have occurred before, causing personal injury.

S: It is true. Before coming to Canada, we rarely heard of peanut allergy in China, but when we came to Canada, every school and every family is important to this kind of thing. Children from other families come to your home to play. Before obtaining the consent of the child's parents, you'd better not give him anything to eat.

It is strictly forbidden to eat food containing nuts such as peanuts in schools. I heard that a child ate peanut butter at home and went to school without brushing his teeth. The classmates smelled the peanut butter and all had allergic reactions.

Y: This may have something to do with the safety of Canadian food. If food is too safe, human immunity will decrease accordingly.

Before giving food, you should also pay attention to the third point: sugar is also the enemy of some special groups, especially diabetics. If you plan to donate food with higher sugar content, you must know in advance whether the recipient can accept it.

Of course, there are some other suggestions. For example, when we donate food to others, we consciously buy those relatively low-priced, large-packaged foods, so that the efficiency of rescue will be higher.

S: What you said is too useful, and there are skills in helping others. If you don't master these skills, the lesser ones will reduce the efficiency of your charity activities, and the more serious ones will even cause you or the recipient's personal and psychological harm.

Y: After a long time, I will naturally consider the problem from the perspective of the recipient, and I can also feel their difficulties. Or to say that this food, if they accept one kind of food for a long time, they can't stand it, so why can they only eat the same kind or the same kind of food?

S: You mentioned a very realistic problem: low-income groups can also be subdivided into categories, and the needs of each category are also diverse. For example, Bill and his charity organization, he seems to mainly help single-parent families.

Y: Yes. I first knew about Bill, it was in 2005, when I was living near his charity organization, and I discovered at that time that he helped many single-parent families, whether it was a single dad or a single mom, he helped. Of course, there are more single mothers. I had just graduated and my income was relatively low. I was a volunteer at another charity that helped single-parent families. I met Bill by the way.

S: The entire Canadian society encourages young people to do volunteer work. To apply for college after graduating from high school, you still have to complete the required volunteer time. You have already graduated and you don't need to accumulate volunteer time to apply for college. You still take the initiative to volunteer, which is really admirable.

Y: Actually, many people, like me, regard volunteering as part of their daily lives. Volunteering in Canada is not something you can do if you want to. It requires interviews, tests, no criminal record, and sometimes some special skills.

For example, the organization where I was a volunteer at the time was mainly to provide children from single-parent families with some normal family experience, which was regarded as a compensatory service. If the child only has a father, the agency will invite a woman to meet with the child regularly, chat, eat, and play, which is equivalent to a temporary mother; if it is the child of a single mother, it will try to find a man to play with the child. This job seems simple, but it is actually very demanding. When I went to apply, after several rounds of interviews, there were various scenario designs, and I had to make plans. For example, take your children to see the plane this week, boating next week, and rescue wild animals next week. How do you arrange these activities, what to prepare, what to pay attention to, what to avoid, and what can your child get? , And so on, if you don't have a little experience, or don't make some preparations in advance, you really won't be able to apply.

S: After you met Bill, did you treat him as the main middleman?

Y: Yes, he is trustworthy, and his charity direction for single-parent families is also my favorite.

Bill does something for charity, he does something, he does not do something, his organization does not accept everything, he does not accept many things. For example, he does not want the most common food for charity organizations; he only accepts clothing and furniture at the beginning, not toys at the beginning, and then slowly adjusts, and then starts accepting some brand new toys.

S: Bill told me that when he first collected clothes, his mother-in-law didn't believe it—how could anyone lack clothes? As soon as his institution opened, his mother-in-law believed that there were indeed many people who lacked the necessary clothes.

Y: This is a very strange or very special phenomenon: some people don't need clothes at all at home, and some people always lack clothes at home. Bill has been keenly observing this from the very beginning, from collecting clothes. Donating clothes to start charity is indeed a very precise direction.

S: Is it because Canada is relatively cold and the four seasons are distinct, so a person needs more clothes? So many low-income families will appear to lack enough clothes?

Y: This must be an important factor. Especially in winter, about half of the time in Canada is winter. If there is not enough warm clothing, it is difficult to survive the winter.

We donated clothes to Bill, a small part of it was old clothes, and most of it was new clothes that we bought and then donated. After all, new clothes are more popular with low-income families. Bill's organization also encourages everyone to donate more new clothes. I consulted Bill, and he said that the recycling rate of used clothes is actually not high. There are quite a lot of clothes collected and sold to mop factories. After the money is exchanged, they will go to charity.

In addition to clothes, another characteristic of Bill's organization is that he has a lot of furniture. Old furniture is also an important charity material.

S: We have a general understanding of this situation. Among furniture, the most popular is the mattress.

Y: Yes, there is a great demand for mattresses, and mattresses are generally new, and the utilization value of old mattresses is too low.

You may not have thought that there is another type of material in the Bill organization that is very popular-diapers that newborns can't live without, which is what we often call diapers. This is what single mothers need most, and they are also the most expensive material. After we had a baby, we felt this firsthand, so we also consciously donated some.

S: We interviewed Bill. He grew up in a single-parent family. His father left them very early. In the most difficult time, his mother could do three jobs at the same time to support the family. When he told these stories, we were all a little awkward: Is this talking about Canada? It has been almost a hundred years since Canada became a developed country.

Y: In fact, this is exactly the value and significance of Bill's charity. Poor people in developed countries are often more likely to be ignored. Doing charity in Oakville, the wealthiest city in Canada, proves that Bill not only has a charitable heart, he also has a smart and profound brain.

Generally, when thinking of charity, top celebrities like to go to the internationally recognized poverty-stricken areas—Africa, like Hollywood stars Angelina Jolie and Brad Pitt; ordinary celebrities like to go to the impoverished areas of their country or region; ordinary people also like to go Relief for the traditionally disadvantaged groups such as the common disabled, the elderly, and orphans; like Bill, to selectively help the neglected local poor in affluent areas is really rare, and it is really very rare.

It has been 16 years since I met Bill in 2005. Bill has been doing the same thing for so many years. This is not easy. It's just like the saying goes; it's not difficult for a person to do a good thing, but the hardest thing is to do good deeds for a lifetime, and not to do bad things. This is the hardest and most difficult thing. Bill has grown from a young man to a middle-aged person. During this period, he has to get married and have a family, raise children, take care of the elderly, and have his own personal life and hobbies. All these things other than charity have not affected him and his charity organization. Normal operation. This is really admirable.

And as we said just now, being a charity in Canada is a very professional thing, and it can't be done with a passion. The use of donated funds, the selection of materials, the recruitment and use of volunteers, the screening of recipients and the auditing statistics of accounts are all very professional work. Without super ability, it cannot be done well and cannot be sustained.

For example, volunteers. I heard that Bill has been using volunteers for many years. At most, there will be dozens of volunteers. The management of these volunteers is very troublesome. It can be promoted by the concept of charity.

S: Let us turn the topic back to you. Canada is a pluralistic society. First nations, European residents, and Asian residents, everyone can live in harmony. You are from China, and you have a high enthusiasm for charity. As far as you know, if there is an average value of charity enthusiasm for Asian residents, especially Chinese residents, is the enthusiasm of Chinese residents to do charity high or low?

Y: Your question is very sharp. I will try to answer it to make sure that the taboo of racial inequality is not touched.

First of all, I think that locals born in Canada have higher enthusiasm and participation in charity than immigrants.

There is an objective reason for this: immigrant groups, whether they are immigrants from China or other countries, will definitely face a difficult period of restarting their lives in the initial stage. During this time, there is still too much time to take care of themselves. I know where I will live next week, so it is difficult to have the ability and energy to help others.

I only came to Canada when I was in college. I had to start over everything and adapt to all kinds of environments. I'm relatively smooth, and there are many other people who have experienced similarly to me, and they have also experienced difficult stages.

Of course, once this difficult stage has passed and the lives of immigrants gradually stabilized, many immigrants will take the initiative to participate in charity activities according to their own strength. Canada is generally a very tolerant and well-intentioned country. When you are in difficulty, when others help you, if you have the ability, you will naturally help others. This is a positive relationship.

As soon as locals are born, most people basically have nothing to worry about. As we said just now, Canada has been a developed country for almost a hundred years. Even a child who grew up in a single-parent family like Bill, his life is difficult no matter how difficult it is. , It is impossible to fall into absolute poverty, it is impossible to experience hunger, but compared with other people, his clothes are relatively less, the food he eats is relatively monotonous, it is a "problem of good and bad", not a The question of "being and not having".

Local residents are more accustomed to doing some charity at any time within the scope of their ability. This is conceivable and is in line with factual logic.

S: This is a well-known saying in China: You know etiquette if you have enough food and clothing. The so-called knowing etiquette must include the virtue of "proactively helping people in difficulties".

Y: Yes, let me go on to the second point. Second, immigrants generally move from developing countries to developed countries. Like the Chinese community, older immigrants generally have experienced the "epoch of material scarcity," and many people have had painful experiences of hunger and cold. After having this experience, there are two different choices: either more stingy, or more generous. Fortunately, the Chinese compatriots I have seen have generally become more generous and generous.

S: Is there a third point?

Y: Of course, the third point: The Chinese community is still an absolute minority in the entire Canadian society. There is no scale and no charity atmosphere. Therefore, many people are still in the stage of consciousness and inaction, and they are soberer, bystander, not a real actor.

S: You are a real actor. You can also bring people around to make the charity atmosphere lively. One last question: Your parents also immigrated to Canada with you. Do they support you in doing charity?

Y: Special support, absolutely support. My mother often reminds me and urges me to help someone. The two of them will go to the elderly gatherings on weekends, which is also called the elderly gathering club. During the gatherings, they will surely hear gossip about the difficulties encountered by each and every one of them. They will remember it in their hearts and they will also know me. My husband and I have a habit of doing charity, so they will give me some tips and let me help a specific person. If you don't see me act when the time comes, they will urge me to go quickly.

S: It seems that your charity awareness and habits have a lot to do with the family you grew up in, and your parents have a great influence on you.

Y: Should it be? The family environment has too much influence on a person. Most of the drug abuse problems we have just mentioned are affected by family members.

Of course, if children are allowed to come into contact with people like Bill earlier, they will be affected by good and normal behavior. As a parent, you can consciously search for such charities. Canadian non-governmental charity activities are very active, and there are many types, and there is a trend of becoming more and more subdivided and more professional.

Just now I mentioned that my father was hospitalized because of illness. At that time, I saw a young mother who was also hospitalized. She had breast cancer and needed chemotherapy. There is an organization that specializes in bringing children to such mothers who need to be hospitalized for chemotherapy. If the mother is not convenient to go to the hospital for chemotherapy, there will be special volunteers to accompany her. The service of this organization is very professional, and the people it serves are also small. They not only take care of people's specific difficulties, but also take care of people's psychological dilemmas. They will provide decompression services to such young mothers and provide psychological counseling to their children, so as to avoid children's psychological problems in the face of such life disasters. It forms a shadow on the surface and creates obstacles to their personality formation.

S: This example can illustrate the problem. It shows that Canadian civil society is very mature and sound. There are people in such a small field who provide highly professional charitable services. The government is not omnipotent. Some governments want to become omnipotent. History and reality have proved that they cannot do it. Only open social charity services, so that social charity forces have enough and sufficient room for development, such very small areas as you mentioned, will be covered by social charity organizations.

Y: Yes, this organization that specializes in serving chemotherapy mothers seems to focus on this field. They will become more professional and more detailed.

Let me give you another example: After my father was discharged from the hospital, the community service organization took the initiative to come to him and arranged for a special person to come to him regularly to bathe him; after a long time, my father even had some dependence and looked forward to volunteering. Come early and help him take a bath. You see, visiting to help elderly patients who are recovering at home after surgery to take a bath is also a subdivided, professional charity event.

Now that the epidemic is not over, many practices that were accustomed to before now have to be re-adjusted to meet the requirements of epidemic prevention. This has also increased the workload of charities including Bill's institutions. I heard that Bill is busier now. Of course, this has something to do with more people being unemployed at home and more families in need after the epidemic.

S: From another perspective, the finer the division of charitable activities and charitable organizations, the easier it is to attract volunteers with special skills to use their expertise and roles.

Y: That's for sure. Nowadays, Internet information is developed, especially the Internet search function. For volunteers, what language do you speak, what ethnic group do you have, what expertise do you have, and how much time can you spend on community service? Once these parameters are entered, you will roughly find suitable charities and volunteer opportunities for you.

In a pluralistic society, everyone is also diverse and has different aspects. It is possible that he is a company employee during the day and a teacher for compulsory education at night; usually he is a corporate executive, and on weekends he goes to charity organizations. It is normal and fun to drive trucks on a voluntary basis. While serving others, you also find partners with the same interests as you, which enriches your life.

S: When the help for disadvantaged groups is

in place, their lives will become richer. We found in Canada that the probability of encountering disabled people, elderly people, and wheelchair travelers on the street is quite high. This is certainly not because there are more disabled people in Canada, but because they are more convenient to travel.

Y: Yes, a disability is of course a misfortune in life, but if you were born in Canada, it would be a blessing in misfortune. Of all the parking lots, the parking spaces for the disabled are always relatively sufficient.

S: Today, by talking about Bill and his organization, we seriously discussed the status quo of charity organizations and charitable activities in Canada. Canadian philanthropy generally has two characteristics, or advantages: one is universality, and the other is individualization.

Y: You sum it up very well. Speaking of universality, I think of another example. Did you know that many of the wards in Canadian hospitals are donated by doctors themselves? Doctors are a high-income group. One of the ways that this group pays back to society is to provide a feature to the hospital, Donate one or several wards.

From a pessimistic perspective, no matter how developed a country is, there are unfortunate individuals and disadvantaged groups. Life is not the worst, only worse; but from an optimistic perspective, the more developed the country and the richer the society, there will be More resources flowing to these unfortunate individuals and disadvantaged groups.

In addition, from a national perspective, Canada, as a developed country, is also doing some cosmopolitan charities that only countries can do internationally: accepting refugees. Over the years, Canada has received a large number of refugees from Syria, Palestine, Venezuela and other war-torn countries or countries with civil conflicts. Canada's generosity and tolerance in this regard is unmatched by any other country.

There are many Chinese friends who seem to be unable to understand the reasons for doing this in Canada. They have made comments on the Internet, criticized or even attacked the refugee policy of the Trudeau government, thinking that so much money should not be spent on refugees. This is taxpayers' money.

I think these people's vision is a bit short-sighted. The reason why Canada has such a developed economy, such a stable society, and such a high international status is directly related to Canada's insistence on actively intervening in international affairs and taking the initiative to assume international responsibilities.

These refugees from Syria, Palestine and other places were unable to guarantee even the most basic living conditions before. After they came to Canada, the government provided them with the most basic living conditions; but this is far from enough. People like Bill and Institutions are all providing some help to refugees who come to the local area. I heard Bill say that recently his inventory of bicycles has almost been distributed, mainly refugee families in Oakville, Burlington, and

Mississauga, where there is too much demand for bicycles.

Since refugees entered Canada, the government and private organizations have been providing relay services. This also reflects a characteristic of Canada: the government and the private sector are jointly governing this society. The government is a limited government, and it will not and cannot take over all affairs; the private sector has a very large degree of autonomy and autonomy, and can make up for the lack and absence of the government as much as possible.

Poverty is unfortunate, but if you are a poor person in a country like Canada, you are lucky in misfortune. Because Canada has people like Bill and many similar charitable organizations, what they do daily is to help the poor in developed countries and in rich cities.

Chapter four

"Please tell everybody about Bill's Safetynet"

——Interview with Safetynet Board Member Katrina Holmes

By Zhaoyan Sun and Zhaohan Sun

Sun(S):   During our last interview with Bill, he told us that the organization has to close down for a while due to financial problems. When you were working as a treasurer, have you ever faced one of those situations?

Katrina(K): I think that happened before I was treasurer, that has not happened since I've been treasurer. Now he(Bill) always has enough money in the bank that he can run the charity for a long time. He could afford to shut down(the charity) for a while; I would say it can last six or seven months while shutted down.

S: Beside working as the treasurer, what type of volunteering are you doing in the charity?

K: I just volunteer on Saturday and Sunday. I sort the clothes, hang up the clothes. I also help with cleaning, sweeping, and organizing the clothes. My job is basically just to make sure the place is neat and tidy for when the next crew comes in.

S: What's the group of people that need the most help within the charity?

K: I don't really know what group of people that need the most help with because I work on the weekends and the charity is close to families on the weekends. I don't really come in contact with a lot of people who use the charity.

S: On the website of Bill's charity, you and your daughter were introduced, how is your daughter doing right now? Is she as enthusiastic about charity as you?

K: My daughter is 26 years old. She lives in Thunder Bay and she works for an airline. Her boyfriend is a pilot. I'm actually going to see her on Saturday for the first time in probably six or seven months. We're going to spend a week together at the cottage so I'm really excited to see her. Yes, she is very supportive of me, and she herself is very enthusiastic about doing some charity.

S: On the website it says that your niece and nephew are also volunteering at a church, what's your thought for them to do volunteer work?

K: I haven't actually brought them since covid-19. I don't feel comfortable bringing them but they've been coming with me since 2017. They used to come every Saturday and help out just to learn. I think volunteering is an important part of everybody's life and I believe everybody should do it. I'm just trying to raise them with the proper values and morals and I believe it's important.

S: Is there a specific reason for you to think that we have to give back to the community more?

K: I think it was my niece and nephew. For me, my life changes started when the whole black lives matter movement started which was about 2017. Since my niece and nephew are black, I felt like I wasn't doing enough to help anybody my whole life. It's just all been for me and my daughter and I just felt like I needed to do more to help people other than myself. I have been and it's changed me as a person really it truly has.

S: What's your perspective on charity work? Are you a fully altruist person or do you think selfishness is good to some extent?

K: I heard this one quote that said you need to fill your cup first whatever overflows is what you get. I do believe that a bit of selfishness is okay. Personally, I take care of myself first because there's no way that I can help anybody else if I'm not okay. I think it's the same in a loving relationship you have to love yourself before you can love anybody else. I do believe that a bit of selfishness is necessary. My cup is full and whatever is overflowing I will give that part to others.

S: Are you satisfied with your current living condition right now?

K: Yes. I had my daughter when I was 19, I was very young, so it's kind of been a stressful life for me. I've been in some good relationships, some bad relationships and now, I think finally I'm able to say that, yes my living conditions, my life is on the right track and I'm very happy.

S: Did your family get affected by the virus outbreak?

K: Nothing, I have nobody who got affected, I don't know anybody who has lost their job. I've been very blessed. Nobody around me has been affected, everybody still has an income. I've been truly blessed.

S: Were you able to help Bill out during this pandemic?

K: I think I'm one of the very few volunteers to continue throughout the pandemic. There's another lady, Shirley, who has gone in almost every single day. She helps empty the bins out for Bill. I still go every single Saturday so I feel like yes I did help him out through the pandemic. I wish I could have done more, however, I have a full time job so there's no way that I could go during the week.

S: Is your current way of volunteering different from the way you used to volunteer?

K: I don't think so. I think other than not seeing as many people on Saturday cuz I'm sorry it's not really busy with all the tutors coming in and out of the students' parents I think other than it just not being that busy it really wasn't any different for me other than having to wear a mask.

S: As a treasurer, which suggestion would you give to other volunteers who're planning to become a treasurer?

K: I think math is very important in school. I'm a big advocate on teaching the kids personal finances in school, and I don't think your child enough about your personal credit on your not taught about compounding interest like you are you're taught how to calculate it, but you're not hot how important it is in your personal finances revolving credit cards loans interest rates that you're paying, you know it's so important especially your credit report like growing up. It's unbelievable how important it is in life to get anywhere in life when it comes to buying a home or buying a car. Your credit score is very important, and we're not taught that in school. so I think I would like to see more of that and I think it's important and staying with you, no running a business running a charity is the same thing you know you have to have more money coming in than you do going out number one rule, so otherwise you will fail so I think that's pretty important.

S: As a volunteer in the charity, have you ever donated to the charity?

K: I donate about $5,000 a year. It's a bonus that I got from work so my bonus from work is about $4,000 and then I probably get about $2,000 of my own money. I truly believe in what he's doing in that charity. It's fantastic and I wish more people knew about it. I wish more people donated. You know I tell people about it all this every chance.

S: The biggest challenge you faced during your career of volunteering?

K: I would say feeling guilty that I don't volunteer enough, I would say that it is my biggest challenge. I wish that I could help him more, I see that especially now during the pandemic he is really struggling, he's struggling emotionally you know because he worries about his family he worries about all of us volunteers, so you know for him to be alone and it's better now because we've hired to volunteers throughout the week, so they're there now to help out but I do wish that I could do more for him.

S: Are you involved in any other charities?

K: No, I donate to some other charities, however, I only volunteer at Bill's SafetyNet. I used to volunteer for a hospital, they have bike races. During the bike race, I would just stand there and hand out water; that's actually how I first started volunteering. I did that for a few months and then I met Bill. so I stopped volunteering at the hospital.

S: Why did you stop volunteering at the hospital?

k: I think they just it was literally just the one thing that they used me for which was the bike races. There was no other volunteer work that they had available other than going around asking people for money. I would literally have to go door-to-door to all businesses and I didn't feel comfortable doing that; it's not the kind of volunteer work that I wanted to do so I left after participating in five or six bike races. I would say this volunteering just isn't fulfilling enough for me, so I didn't feel like I was doing anything specific for the hospital. That's why I left the hospital.

S: If you were to leave a comment on SafetyNet, what comment would you write?

K: I would literally write please tell everybody about this charity. Literally everybody needs to know about it and everybody needs to donate. I'm sure there's more people who could use our services but really don't know that we're available. We have so many people come on the weekends to drop stuff off and say, "I didn't even know that you exist." I think Bill right now is trying to get the word out there, he's using social media a lot more. I think that is the one comment I would say, "tell everybody."

S: How much time do you spend volunteering at the charity?

K: It takes me about 20 minutes each way so maybe an hour driving every weekend. So I guess it's about 5 or 6 hours per weekend. Then I spent about hours 3 or 4 hours a month doing the treasurer job plus the board meeting. I would say a total of 30 hours a month.

S: Do you want your niece and nephew to follow your footsteps?

K: Yes, I think my niece will do such volunteering and my nephew right now would rather play. My niece definitely has learned a lot from underprivileged families and she now understands her privilege. She now understands that not every family is like her family. I do think that young children need to be more aware of work and what you are doing.

S: Do you think that the government should do more to help the charity?

K: It's hard to say because I am definitely a socialist when it comes to helping people but I also have the mindset that money just can't doesn't come off trees. So at the end of the day, yes, we can count on the government to help us out. However, we are going to be the one to have your taxes through. I am of the mindset that we need to be going to the community and asking for donations rather than depending on the government to help us, that's my personal opinion. I think the government does help a lot, we have a lot of programs like the clothing and furniture banks subsidized by the government. They give us money for every bed that we deliver. There are a lot of government assistant programs.

The government helped me when I was a single mom at 19 years old, they helped me get on my feet and I appreciated it very much. However, I think there is a time when the government just cannot support everybody.

S: As a single mother, what's the thing that you needed the most?

K: I would say I needed my mom the most, my mom and my sister. That's what I needed the most. In terms of materials, I would say food and diapers are what I needed the most. Food and diapers were the most expensive thing. Diapers are so expensive even back then they were. Diapers are even more expensive now, I don't know how some people make it through. The cost of everything is triple from 26 years ago.

S: What's your most memorable moment at this charity?

K: So there's one gentleman Abdel, he was a Syrian refugee and he now volunteers at the charity. One day he came and told me the story about how this car got towed he's just parked at the parking lot and ran across the street he came back with his kids and the car was gone, so he called his number and they told him that his car was towed, and the guy brought back to his car tow truck driver, and then charged and hearing the story and seeing this man who is working his ass off to support his family for his children. I just know he does not have the $400 to get his car back, so I went and raised $400 for him, and I gave the money to Bill. Next time I saw him, he told me that he doesn't really know how to say it in

English, but there has to be a word that is more meaningful than thank you, and you know to do that. Such an amazing person like he is truly one of the nicest people I've ever met, and you see something that horrible happened to him, it just really angered me, so it was I think one of my most memorable things I will never forget it.

Chapter five

"Volunteering makes me feel grounded"

——Interview with Board Member and secretary
Sophia Grochmal

By Zhaoyan Sun and Zhaohan Sun

Sun(S): When did you start volunteering? What type of volunteer did you first do?

Grochmal(G):   I started volunteering in 2017. I started helping with sorting clothes and organizing the charity. Back then I occasionally helped them(the charity) to pick up the phone but not too often.

S: Is SafetyNet the first charity you worked for?

G: Yeah, I did some research because I wanted to help out the community. It's also because my children are getting older so I wanted to be a good role model for them. And I ended up choosing SafetyNet because that's where I think I can make the most impact.

S: What made you stay at SafetyNet? What do you like most about SafetyNet?

G: I really like the idea of handing out clothing for free in SafetyNet. Donated clothing doesn't just go to recycle and people don't need to pay for it, I think this is why I chose to stay.

S: On the website, it also says that you work for MS(Multiple Sclerosis) society, what's the major difference between the two organizations you work for?

G: My link to the MS society is that both my mother and my husband's mother have MS. For many years we tried to treat it through walking and fundraising; I raised my money in the MS society, they spent that money through research. I would say the major difference is that MS society is helping people in the long term, but SafetyNet is like a day to day thing.

S: How much time do you spend working on each of those two charities during a week?

G: It's hard for me to answer that question now because I have taken a step back in recent years from SafetyNet in the day to day operation. I have to do this because I have gone back to work in fall. However, I'm still involved in both the MS society and SafetyNet. It's just that I spent a lot more time before.

S: According to the SafetyNet website, you work for the clothing department. What's the biggest challenge that you faced in the clothing department?

Recently I can't think of any, but before there was a problem of having not enough teenage clothing. We had enough for adults and babies, however, we were short on teenage clothing. Nowadays, we don't need to worry about that, we are always in need of whatever is required.

S: What's the biggest challenge you faced during your volunteer time?

G: The biggest challenge I had to deal with is the different personalities different identity volunteers have. That's the biggest challenge I faced during my career of volunteering.

S: Are the volunteers you met in SafetyNet easy to be friends with?

G: I feel like they are, I haven't met anyone who's super hard to deal with yet.

S: When you first got involved with volunteering, were you surprised by the number of people who need help? especially in a wealthy town like Oakville?

G: Definitely, the need that's there really surprised me. For me, I think the percentage will be a lot lower; there's a lot of refugees that need help as well. Before you actually get involved in those kinds of services, you don't realize how many people need help in Oakville.

S: How did the COVID-19 virus outbreak affect your volunteering?

G: Well, Bill has to run the organization on his own for safety reasons. We shut down other than diaper services. We were shut down for quite a while and I think it's been really hard for him.

S: Were you able to help Bill remotely?

G: No, there's not much me and the other volunteers can do for him.

S: What suggestions would you give to new volunteers that will help them with volunteering?

G: Some suggestions I would give is to ask questions when in need and try to handle oneself because of charity like people who have good self-management.

S: What's your relationship with Bill? How did you become the secretary of this charity organization?

G: We have a solid relationship; we have a company business that helps SafetyNet. We have a good and open relationship so we can talk about anything. How did I come on board? I was involved when I first started volunteering, I really enjoyed it. Bill at the time had a different board and the secretary had stepped down so he was looking for someone who can handle the job. I was so involved back then so I later became the new secretary in 2017.

S: How do you manage the Board of Directors in this organization? Were there a lot of disagreements when it comes to a discussion?

G: We have a monthly meeting, and there's a lot of rules and regulations on the board. The members try their best to follow the rule. Usually, we set an agenda the week before then everyone has time to think about what they are going to say about. We can take a vote if necessary. The current virus outbreak did affect our meeting a little bit because we can't really meet everyone in contact.

S: Is your family supportive of you doing this type of volunteering?

G: Yeah, definitely.

S: Could you talk about your family in terms of volunteering?

G: My oldest child volunteers at SafetyNet and my other children are too young to do things like that. They sometimes come with me to SafetyNet but it's not a regular thing.

S: As a volunteer of SafetyNet, have you ever donated to the charity?

G: No, I never donated money to SafetyNet, however, I donated material goods like items of clothing.

S: Does religion have an impact on what you're doing right now?

G: I think it does have some indirect impact on me. I'm not doing charity work because I'm a Roman catholic. I think I do it because of the way I was brought up and the principles form my religion. I feel like I have to get back to the community however, it's not directly due to my religion.

S: What is your perspective on charitable work, are you a fully autistic person or do you think selfishness is good to some extent?

G: I think that I'm in the middle of the two ideologies. I don't think selfishness is good, however, I need to take care of myself before helping others. You should take care of yourself before you worry about others.

S: During your time at college, were you involved in any political event? (Bill told us that he was involved in some of the events.)

G: No, I have not. Not at all. I got into charity work at that time though.

S: While being active in charity, where does your salary come from? In other words, how do you ensure your living?

G: As I said before, I went full-time back to work in my family company. I ensure my living this way.

S: Was there a time when you wanted to quit volunteering because it's such a challenge for you?

G: Not for me, it's the opposite of what you said. When I'm having a bad day, I go to the charity to volunteer and turn my day around. I think that's what more I get from it. I think volunteering makes me feel grounded, the conversations I had with the people I help really help me get out of the bad mood.

S: How did your family get affected by the virus outbreak?

G: Well, it has been a tough time for our business since people don't want to have contact with us. But other than that, it barely affected my family. I don't think that part affected us differently than other families.

S: What do you think SafetyNet could improve on in the future?

G: Because I'm not involved in the day-to-day service anymore, so it's hard for me to answer. I really can't think of one area they could improve on.

Chapter Six

——Interview with Chil

By Zhaoyan Sun and Zhaohan Sun

Sun(S):   How much time do you spend volunteering a week?

Chill(C):   10-12 hours a week generally, That's an average, sometimes I don't show up and other times I volunteer way more than I need to be.

S: Do you have certain days in the week where you show up in the week, or do you not have a fixed schedule?

C: I generally show up in the evening, and I try to show up twice a week. It used to depend on my schedule because I had a shift job, so whenever I have the energy I will come in to help the Charity(SafetyNet). As for the past year and a half, I've been promoted to a day job, thus I can come in more regularly after then. But generally, I come in usually in the evening anyway, so let's just say that I come in on Monday, Wednesday, and Saturday most often.

S: Have you ever volunteered at charities other than SafetyNet?

C: Yeah, I used to volunteer at the Oakville Trafalgar Hospital, I did that during high school and after university for a total time period of five years total. I also volunteered at a bike shop, and I did this for 4-5 years. However, the atmosphere there for me was very casual, I showed up to the shop once in a week maybe.

Other trivial things that sort of count as volunteering. I also volunteered for some weird stuff during high school, long story short I did a lot of "odd" volunteering.

S: Under the circumstances of this virus outbreak, are you still able to help the charity?

C: Yes, I'm working at home, I use zoom for meetings and for work. SafetyNet, I'm lucky, because they promoted me as the guy in charge of all bikes. It's actually the best place for me to go(the bike house), because when I go to the charity at night, no one else is there. Bill gave me the key years ago because he knew that I often come at night and I will need a key. So I'm still volunteering, still 10 hours a day right now even.

S: Why did you choose to stay working in this Charity for years?

C: Because it's the only non-religious related charity in Oakville. I'm just doing bike riding for the community, and it's really that aspect that I enjoy the most: the general goodwill. I think another reason why I stayed here is that Bill is a nice guy, really open to new ideas. Originally I just came here to fix the bikes, you know just pump the tires and clean them. But as times passed on, he gave me a lot of freedom, and this year I pretty much turned it from a pile of bikes into a bike shop. We got some sponsors and a lot more bikes, and now the back of this warehouse is just full of bikes now. And on top of that, we have four volunteers just for the bike section, that's quite a group now. Yeah and back to what I was talking about, Bill gave me a lot of free decisions and trust.

S: Now the bikes in this charity are sort of like the unique feature and the biggest part of the charity as Bill said last time during our interview.

C: Yeah, the bike section is growing really fast right now, and the bike is a field where it requires a lot of expertise to be honest. And I think people like our bikes in this charity because there's not a lot of free bike shops here. I know another charity which also provides bikes but the scale of it is very small. They only had 20-50 bikes, on the other hand, our charity just by myself had fixed over 150 bikes during the 4 months of summer. It's been a good year.

S: How the pandemic affected your work and volunteering?

C: Since I'm working for healthcare here, I and other fellows just work harder than usual for this pandemic. My day job from Toronto can be done online and that's really nice. And we are just busy because COVID is keeping us really really busy, thousands of tests per day, now ten thousand per day. In terms of volunteering, Bill and other people are doing the Furniture part and I'm doing the bike section. In that sense, the charity has stabilized.

S: Have you helped out the charity in other ways? For example, such as donating and advertising?

C: In general, I do donate and raise money for this charity and other charities. And I do some advertising here and there, I don't advertise through social media though. I just tell people that I meet every day about this charity in a casual way. And for my job, I do try to contact everyone to notice that they have work/meetings.

S: If you have to make a choice between donation and volunteering, which one do you think is more important?

C: I think, fundamentally, volunteering is more important. And It's up to the individual to work together to improve society. But I mean donation is also important.

S: How much time do you spend volunteering a week?

C: 10-12 hours a week generally, That's an average, sometimes I don't show up and other times I volunteer way more than I need to be.

S: Do you have certain days in the week where you show up in the week, or do you not have a fixed schedule?

C: I generally show up in the evening, and I try to show up twice a week. It used to depend on my schedule because I had a shift job, so whenever I have energy I will come in to help the Charity(SafetyNet). As for the past year and a half I've been promoted to a daytime job, thus I can come in more regularly after then. But generally I come in usually in the evening anyway, so let's just say that I come in on Monday, Wednesday, and Saturday most often.

S: Have you ever volunteered at other charities other than SafetyNet?

C: Yeah, I used to volunteer at the Oakville Trafalgar Hospital, I did that during high school and after university for a total time period of five years total. I also volunteered at a bike shop, and I did this for 4-5 years. However, the atmosphere there for me was very casual, I showed up to the shop once in a week maybe. Other trivial things that sort of count as volunteering. I also volunteered for some weird stuff during high school, long story short I did a lot of "odd" volunteering.

S: Under the circumstances of this virus outbreak, are you still able to help the charity?

C: Yes, I'm working at home, I use zoom for meetings and for work. SafetyNet, I'm lucky, because they promoted me as the guy in charge of all bikes. It's actually the best place for me to go (to the bike house), because when I go to the charity at night, no one else is there. Bill gave me the key years ago because he knew that I often come at night and I will need a key. So I'm still volunteering, still 10 hours a day right now even.

Made in the USA
Monee, IL
20 December 2021

86477294R10090